Beginner's Guide to Python Programming

Learn Python Fundamentals, Plotting and Tkinter GUI Development Easily

Serhan Yamacli

Manchester Academic Publishers

Beginner's Guide to Python Programming – First Edition

This book is dedicated to Guido van Rossum...

Table of Contents

Part I. Python Basics

Chapter 1. Introduction

Welcome to your guide to Python programming.

This compact book aims to teach Python programming language assuming that the reader does not have any programming experience. You don't need to have any software development experience to learn the concepts and projects presented in this book. I'll assume that you have no knowledge on programming and software development. I'll try to explain every bit of Python programming with plain words and will try to make things easy to understand. This book will take you as a beginner and at the end of the book; you'll be able to create your Python programs with graphical user interfaces (GUIs) with plotting and other capabilities. By the way, I'd like to remind you that a single book cannot make you an expert on a subject. However, this book will teach you a lot on Python programming and you'll have a solid background to learn more afterwards.

1.1. Why Python?

Why is it a good idea to learn Python? I'm sure you have your own good reasons. Mine were as the following:

1. It's because Python is probably the easiest programming language to learn nowadays.
2. We can develop a wide range of software such as games, web applications and scientific programs using Python.
3. Python is free and open source. And thousands of people contribute to this beautiful language.
4. Programming in Python is fun and there is usually a practical "Pythonic way" of realizing a software algoritm in Python.
5. Python is the very popular programming language according to the TIOBE index (https://www.tiobe.com/tiobe-index/) which means that learning Python will definitely contribute to your CV.

1.2.   What you will learn in this book?

You will learn the following subjects using this book:

- Fundamentals of the Python programming language: basic and advanced data types,
- Conditional statements and loops in Python,
- Writing our of functions and classes in Python,
- Writing and using modules in Python,
- Database operations using Python
- Developing our graphical user interface (i.e. windowed) programs in Tkinter.

1.3.   Who this book is for?

In my opinion this book is especially ideal for:

- Complete beginners in a programming language or in Python,
- Those who know another language and want to learn the Python syntax and the Pythonic way of programming,
- Beginner or intermediate level Python programmers who want to learn databases,
- Python programmers who want to learn developing software with GUIs.

1.4.   The teaching method used in this book

Programming languages can only be learnt by practicing a lot as in the spoken languages. Therefore we will apply the following method in each of the chapters:

- I'll show you the fundamentals of the subject
- We'll do practical examples together
- I'll give you some exercises which will motivate you to practice your knowledge (I personally dislike dealing with difficult exercises when I just start to learn something new so I'll not give difficult exercises until the end of the book)

I'm sure you'll be able to say "I know Python programming" after you finish this book by looking back to see the programs you created during your Python education.

1.5.   The book's companion website

This book has a companion website at www.yamaclis.com/python. You can download all the project files, Python source files and high-resolution versions of the images of the book form this companion website. You can also make public comments and ask questions on the forum there.

1.6.   Contact information

Learning a programming language is not an easy thing therefore it is completely normal to have questions while following this book. Please drop me an e-mail at syamacli@gmail.com to ask your questions and I'll be happy to help you. Alternatively, you can ask your questions at my website www.yamaclis.com/python if you'd like to share your questions and opinions publicly.

Please come and join us in this book to discover the wonders offered by Python!

Chapter 2. Installing Python

There are numerous development environments for Python as in other languages. Development environment means an integrated software consisted of an advanced text editor which automatically highlights our source code (the text file in which we write our program), a compiler/interpreter and a module called debugger which helps finding programming errors. PyCharm from Jetbrains and PyDev that is integrated inside the famous Eclipse. We can always use any development tool once we grasp the basics of Python. Since the aim of this book is to start learning Python swiftly, we will start our learning journey using *the official Python development environment, IDLE,* and then install more advanced development environments in the upcoming parts of the book when we need them.

2.1. The Python integrated development and learning environment: IDLE

Python IDLE is a software in which we can try our Python code in real time or write complex code inside a highlighted editor. Please navigate to the official Python homepage (https://www.python.org/) and then navigate to the Downloads section as shown in Figures 2.1 and 2.2. There are various choices in the Downloads section. The main choice is for the main Python version. Our alternatives are Python 3.x and Python 2.x (here x denotes the secondary version indicators). The coding rules for Python 3.x and Python 2.x are different and they are not compliant meaning that the code you write in Python 2.x will not run on Python 3.x and vice versa. Since the current version of the Python is Python 3, I'll teach you thic version in this book. The current Python version is Python 3.6.5 as seen in Figure 2.2. Please click the Download Python 3.6.5 button on this web page to initiate downloading the installer for the currrent version of Python.

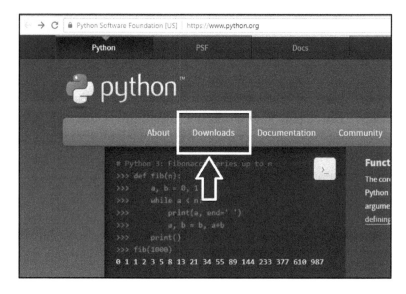

Figure 2.1. The Python homepage

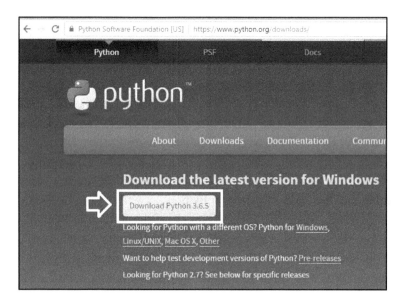

Figure 2.2. Download section

Please note that you may need to select a different Python installer if you're using Mac or Linux. Please follow the links at the end of the *Looking for Python with a different OS?* section.

The installer file named python-3.6.5.exe will be downloaded in this step (the secondary numbers might be changed at the time you're reading here but that's not important as long as the main version is Python 3). Double-click this installer once it has finished downloading. It shouldn't take long to download since it's only about 30MB (the Pythonic way- small, simplei functional). The following installation window will appear. Firstly, check the *Add Python 3.6 to PATH* checkbox as indicated by number 1 below:

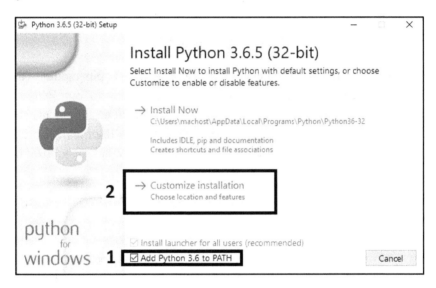

Figure 2.3. Python installation window

Python will be installed in the path (in the folder) given by C:\Users\username\AppData\ Programs\Python\Python36-32 as you can see from the above figure. You can install to any location on your computer but I personally prefer a simpler folder such as C:\Python36. If you agree with me, click the *Customize installation* button as shown by number 2 in the above figure. The customisation options shown in will appear:

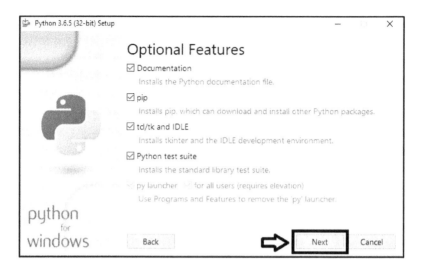

Figure 2.4. Customising installation (1)

We are OK with the documentation (the help files), pip module (the module which helps installing additional capabilities to our Python), tcl/tk (Tkinter GUI library and the IDLE development environment) and the Python test suite (as the name indicates, testing libraries). We can click *Next* and then we'll be presented with the second customization window:

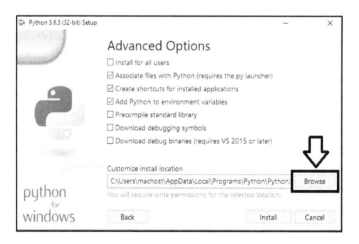

Figure 2.5. Customising installation (2)

Please click the *Browse* button to select the folder in which you want to install your Python interpreter, IDLE and default libraries. I have created a folder as C:\Python36 and selected it as shown below:

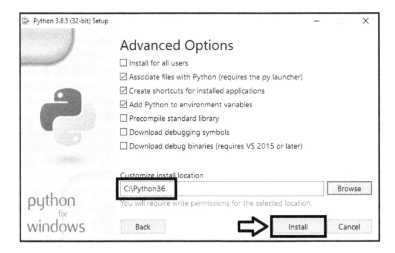

Figure 2.6. Selecting the installation folder

We can now click the *Install* button to start installation of Python with these options. The installation will be completed in a short time and it will say Installation was successful. We can now close the installation window:

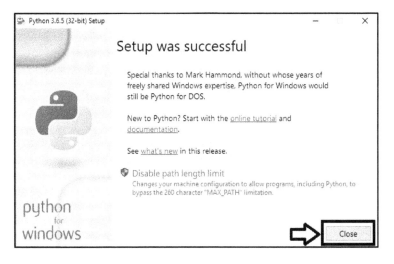

Figure 2.7. Successful installation of Python 3

We have now installed Python on our computer and ready to go for learning Python programming language. But before that, let's overview the installed components. Please navigate to the folder in which you installed Python (C:\Python36 if you followed the above method):

DLLs	12.06.2018 15:48	
Doc	12.06.2018 15:48	
include	12.06.2018 15:48	
Lib	12.06.2018 15:48	
libs	12.06.2018 15:48	
Scripts	12.06.2018 15:49	
tcl	12.06.2018 15:49	
Tools	12.06.2018 15:48	
LICENSE.txt	28.03.2018 16:14	30 KB
NEWS.txt	28.03.2018 16:14	384 KB
python.exe	28.03.2018 16:11	96 KB
python3.dll	28.03.2018 16:08	58 KB
python36.dll	28.03.2018 16:08	3.226 KB
pythonw.exe	28.03.2018 16:11	95 KB
vcruntime140.dll	9.06.2016 22:46	82 KB

Figure 2.8. The Python installation structure

We don't need to know everything about these files of course. But it is good to know something about the Python's structure. The main Python file is the python.exe, which is the Python interpreter. When we write a Python program, we send our program file to this interpreter. The interpreter knows a lot of things about our computer and operating system and executes our Python program with its wisdom. Therefore, we shouldn't delete it if we want to execute Python programs on our computer. Another important file is the IDLE development tool located at C:\Python36\Lib\idlelib. We can access IDLE also from the start menu (Windows Key->All programs -> IDLE). When we run IDLE, it appears as shown in Figure 2.9.

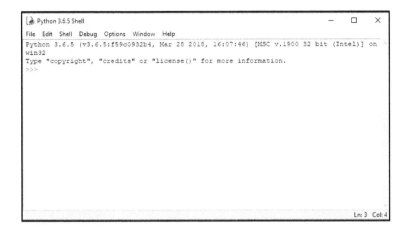

Figure 2.9. The IDLE (**I**ntegrated **D**evelopment and **L**earning **E**nvironment) window

2.2. The "Hello World" example

We can write our Python commands in this IDLE window and get its result instantly. The >>> of the IDLE is its command prompt line and waiting your input at that prompt. For example, let's write our first Python command: print("Hello World") at the IDLE prompt:

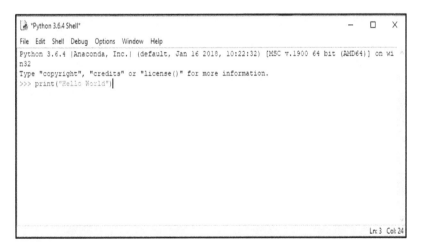

Figure 2.10. Using the IDLE prompt

As you'll see from your IDLE, the Python command will automatically be coloured making us easier to follow the code. This is the classical

Hello World example meaning that we just write Hello World on the screen to verify that our Python installation is working correctly. After writing our command at the IDLE prompt, we need to press Enter on the keyboard to send this command to the Python interpreter for it to execute this command. When we press Enter, we tell the Python interpreter to print the statement inside the parantheses on the screen as follows:

```
Python 3.6.4 Shell                                           —   □   ×
File  Edit  Shell  Debug  Options  Window  Help
Python 3.6.4 |Anaconda, Inc.| (default, Jan 16 2018, 10:22:32) [MSC v.1900 64 bit (AMD64)] on wi
n32
Type "copyright", "credits" or "license()" for more information.
>>> print("Hello World")
Hello World
>>> |

                                                             Ln: 5  Col: 4
```

Figure 2.11. Executing our first command at the IDLE prompt

The Hello World text displayed in blue at the IDLE window is the output of our Python interpreter. (Please remember that you can download the high-resolution colour versions of these figures from the book's compainon website: www.yamaclis.com/python.) If you see this output, congratulations. Your Python installation is working fine and we are ready to continue to Chapter 3 where we will see the variable types in Python.

Chapter 3. Variables in Python

We will learn the basics of Python in this chapter including variables, string operations and basic input/output commands.

3.1. Variables: What is a variable in programming?

Variables are entities that hold information. You can think them as boxes that you put and get data into and from them. There are several types of variables exist in Python and we will learn them in this chapter.

In some programming languages such as C and Java, variable types have to be declared before using them and cannot be changed throught the program. This is called statically typing. However, in some other languages like Python, variables are dynamically typed meaning that we do not have to specify the variable type, we just assign the variable and the Python interpreter automatically assigns the variable type internally. We can also change the variable type in Python whenever we need to. Another reason to love Python!

3.2. Integer variables

This is the same as integers in mathematics. The numbers without a floating point are considered as integers in Python. Integers can be negative, positive or zero such as 12, 3473, -34, 0, 18373920383. There is no limit for the magnitude of integers in Python programmatically (of course limited by the PC's memory:)). We can simply define an integer variable by giving it a name and using the equal sign. Let's define the number of days in a week in Python:

```
number_of_days=7
```

It's this simple in Python. We have created a variable called number_of_days and assigned 7 to it. It's like we put 7 inside the number_of_days box:

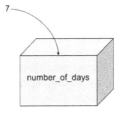

Figure 3.1. The variable number_of_days can be thought as a box

Just write our statement number_of_days=7 and press Enter on the keyboard in the IDLE to give this command to Python:

```
Python 3.5.2 Shell                                    —    □    ×
File  Edit  Shell  Debug  Options  Window  Help
Python 3.5.2 (v3.5.2:4def2a2901a5, Jun 25 2016, 22:18:55) [MSC v.1900
64 bit (AMD64)] on win32
Type "copyright", "credits" or "license()" for more information.
>>> number_of_days=7
>>> |
```

Figure 3.2. Creating and assigning an integer variable

We created the variable in Python. We can simply write the name of the variable in the IDLE again and Python will show its contents (note that IDLE has code completion, if you just write a few letters such as numb and hit the Tab button on your keyboard IDLE will complete it as number_of_days):

```
Python 3.5.2 Shell                                    —    □    ×
File  Edit  Shell  Debug  Options  Window  Help
Python 3.5.2 (v3.5.2:4def2a2901a5, Jun 25 2016, 22:18:55) [MSC v.1900
64 bit (AMD64)] on win32
Type "copyright", "credits" or "license()" for more information.
>>> number_of_days=7
>>> number_of_days
7
>>> |
```

Figure 3.3. Checking the contents of our variable

The contents of our variable is now stored somewhere on our computer's volatile memory, i.e. RAM. If you close IDLE and open it and then ask for the contents of the variable, it will say that variable is not defined:

```
Python 3.5.2 Shell                                    —    □    ✕
File  Edit  Shell  Debug  Options  Window  Help
Python 3.5.2 (v3.5.2:4def2a2901a5, Jun 25 2016, 22:18:55) [MSC v.
1900 64 bit (AMD64)] on win32
Type "copyright", "credits" or "license()" for more information.
>>> number_of_days
Traceback (most recent call last):
  File "<pyshell#0>", line 1, in <module>
    number_of_days
NameError: name 'number_of_days' is not defined
>>>
```

Figure 3.4. The variable is erased when we restart IDLE

Anyway, let's define number_of_days again if you restrated the IDLE and see what we can do with it. First of all as you may have noted that we can use underscore in the variable names. However we cannot use most of the special symbols such as : , ? , (,) , = , - , etc. Therefore it is a good practice to get used to using underscore when our variable name consists of more than one word. Also remember that a variable name cannot start with a number.

As we have defined our variable, let's ask its type to Python. We will use a built-in function called type() for this. We'll write the name of the variable as the argument inside the parantheses:

```
type(number_of_days)
```

Python responds as <class 'int'> as you can see from your IDLE and Figure 3.5. It means the variable is derived from the integer class as shown in Figure 3.5.

```
Python 3.5.2 Shell                                    —    □    ✕
File  Edit  Shell  Debug  Options  Window  Help
Python 3.5.2 (v3.5.2:4def2a2901a5, Jun 25 2016, 22:18:55) [MSC v.190
0 64 bit (AMD64)] on win32
Type "copyright", "credits" or "license()" for more information.
>>> number_of_days=7
>>> type(number_of_days)
<class 'int'>
>>>
```

Figure 3.5. Asking the variable type using the type() function

We can use the usual mathematical operators on the integer variables such as addition (+), subtraction (-), multiplication (*) and division (/). Let's calculate the number of days in 2 weeks with both the addition and the multiplication operators:

```
new_var=number_of_days + number_of_days
```

or

```
new_var=2*number_of_days
```

Here we defined a new variable called new_var. It will have the value of 14 after one of these operations as shown in Figure 3.6.

Note that we don't need to create a new variable to do mathematical operations on integers. For example we can just write:

```
number_of_days-2
```

and press Enter and Python would give the result as 5 as shown in Figure 3.7.

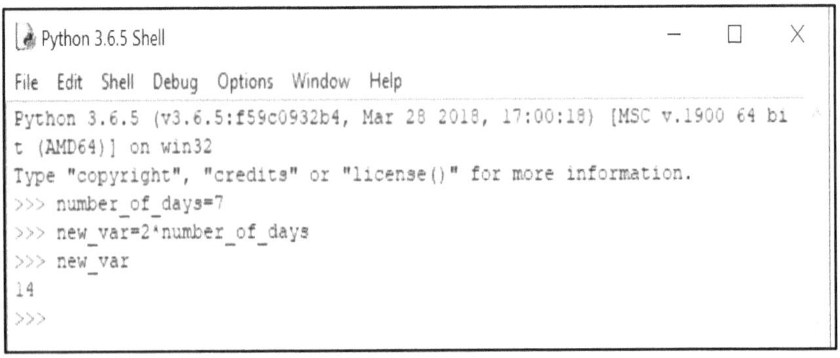

Figure 3.6. Multiplication operation

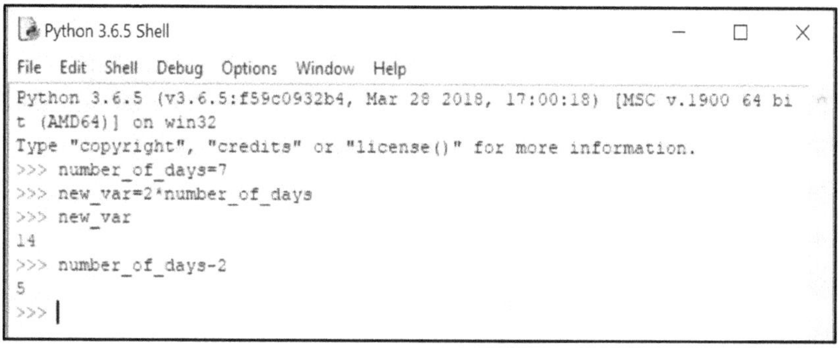

Figure 3.7. Real-time subtraction operation

An important property of the variables is that we can update their values. For example if we want to store the number of days in a year in our number_of_days variable, we just assign it again to 365 as shown in Figure 3.8.

```
number_of_days=365
```

In programming, we sometimes need to update the value of the integers using its current value. I mean we may need to decrease or increase the variable's value. For example, let's increase the value of our number_of_days variable by one. For this, we will use the expression:

```
number_of_days=number_of_days+1
```

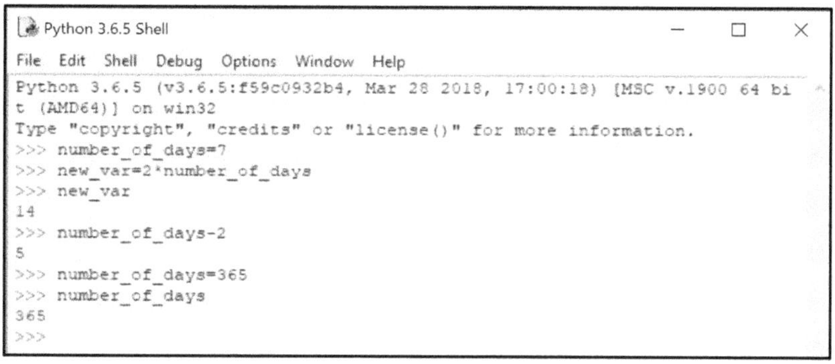

Figure 3.8. Updating a variable's value

This means that the variable number_of_days will be increased by 1 and then the new value will be assigned to this variable back. The current value of this variable is 365. Let's execute the above expression in IDLE and ask for the content of the variable again as shown in Figure 3.9. As you can see, the value of the variable is now 366 as expected. We can of course use other mathematical operators also for updating a variable's value. For example, if we use the following command in IDLE, it will multiply the value of the number_of_days variable and assign it back to itself:

```
number_of_days =number_of_days*2
```

Our number_of_days variable has the value of 366 before this operation. After this operation, it will have the value of 366*2=732 as shown in Figure 3.10.

There are also shortened expressions for updating a variable's value. We use the required operator followed by the equal sign. For example, we can increment the value of our variable by 2 using the following expression:

```
number_of_days += 2
```

This expression is equivalent to:

```
number_of_days = number_of_days+2
```

as you can see in IDLE in Figure 3.11.

```
Python 3.6.5 Shell                                    —    □    ×
File  Edit  Shell  Debug  Options  Window  Help
Python 3.6.5 (v3.6.5:f59c0932b4, Mar 28 2018, 16:07:46) [MSC v.1900 32
bit (Intel)] on win32
Type "copyright", "credits" or "license()" for more information.
>>> number_of_days=7
>>> new_var=2*number_of_days
>>> new_var
14
>>> number_of_days-2
5
>>> number_of_days=365
>>> number_of_days
365
>>> number_of_days=number_of_days+1
>>> number_of_days
366
>>> |



                                                          Ln: 15  Col: 4
```

Figure 3.9. Updating the variable's value – addition

```
Python 3.6.5 Shell                                    —    □    ×
File  Edit  Shell  Debug  Options  Window  Help
Python 3.6.5 (v3.6.5:f59c0932b4, Mar 28 2018, 16:07:46) [MSC v.1900 32
bit (Intel)] on win32
Type "copyright", "credits" or "license()" for more information.
>>> number_of_days=7
>>> new_var=2*number_of_days
>>> new_var
14
>>> number_of_days-2
5
>>> number_of_days=365
>>> number_of_days
365
>>> number_of_days=number_of_days+1
>>> number_of_days
366
>>> number_of_days=number_of_days*2
>>> number_of_days
732
>>>

                                                          Ln: 18  Col: 4
```

Figure 3.10. Updating the variable's value - multiplication

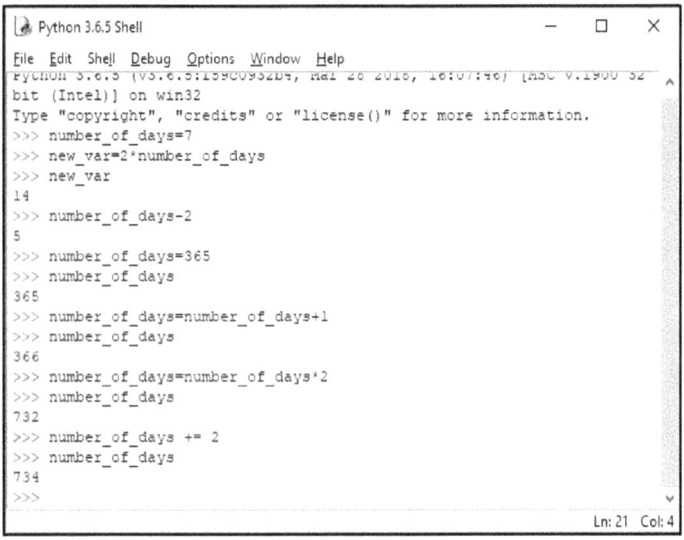

Figure 3.11. The shortened expression for adding 2

3.3. Floating point variables

In mathematics, we express the numbers with fractional parts using the floating point. For example, we can express the pi number as 3.14 (approximately). The float type in Python just stores the numbers with fractional parts as in maths. Let's define the pi to be 3.14 in Python:

```
pi=3.14
```

Note that we use the point not comma for seperating the integer and fractional parts.

Let's try this in IDLE as in Figure 3.12.

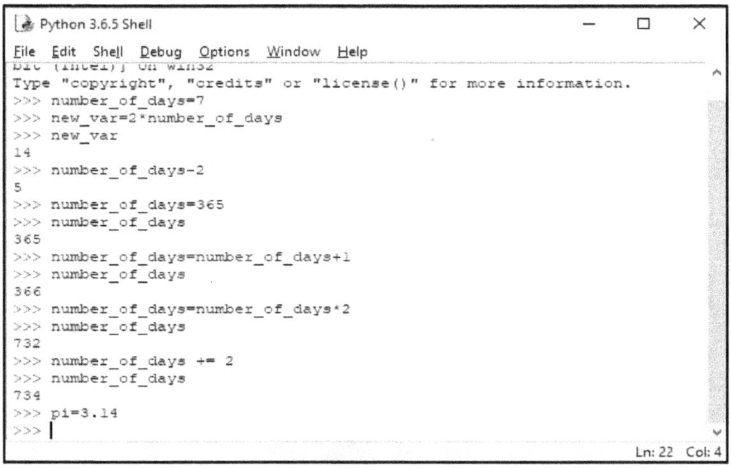

```
Python 3.6.5 Shell                                          —    □    ×
File  Edit  Shell  Debug  Options  Window  Help
bit (intel)] on win32
Type "copyright", "credits" or "license()" for more information.
>>> number_of_days=7
>>> new_var=2*number_of_days
>>> new_var
14
>>> number_of_days-2
5
>>> number_of_days=365
>>> number_of_days
365
>>> number_of_days=number_of_days+1
>>> number_of_days
366
>>> number_of_days=number_of_days*2
>>> number_of_days
732
>>> number_of_days += 2
>>> number_of_days
734
>>> pi=3.14
>>> |
                                                         Ln: 22  Col: 4
```

Figure 3.12. Defining a float type in Python

Let's use this approximate pi to calculate the area of a circle with the radius of 2:

```
r=2
area=pi*r*r
```

The IDLE will give the correct answer as expected:

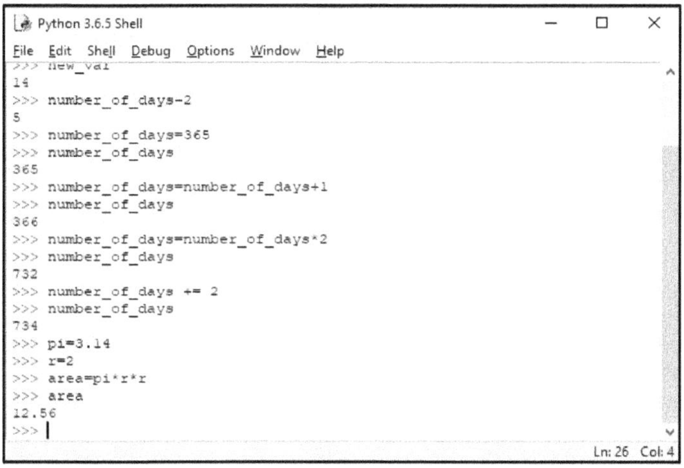

```
Python 3.6.5 Shell                                          —    □    ×
File  Edit  Shell  Debug  Options  Window  Help
>>> new_var
14
>>> number_of_days-2
5
>>> number_of_days=365
>>> number_of_days
365
>>> number_of_days=number_of_days+1
>>> number_of_days
366
>>> number_of_days=number_of_days*2
>>> number_of_days
732
>>> number_of_days += 2
>>> number_of_days
734
>>> pi=3.14
>>> r=2
>>> area=pi*r*r
>>> area
12.56
>>> |
                                                         Ln: 26  Col: 4
```

Figure 3.13. Using the float and integer types together

Note that we have used the integer (r) and float (pi) types together in this operation. The output is also of float type (area). In general, the result will be of float type when a float type is inside the operation. On the other hand, the result of two integers may also be of float type as follows:

```
a=2
b=3
c=a/b
```

Let's try this in Python:

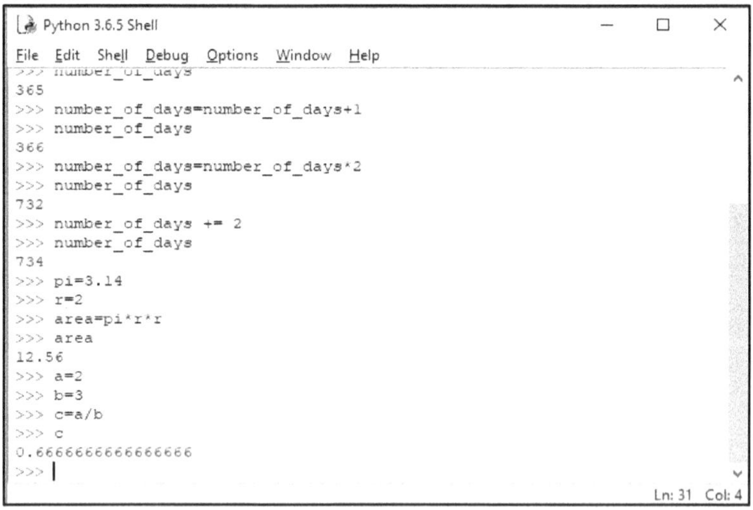

Figure 3.14. The result of the division of two integers as float

Python is a great language! It automatically manages the types.If you have used or will use other statically typed languages, you'll see that this type management phenomena is very helpful.

3.4. Basic mathematical operators

There are lots of them in Python and we will now see more of them here.

3.4.1. The addition operator: +

As we have seen before, we just apply this operator as in usual maths:

```
a=2
b=3
c=a+b
```

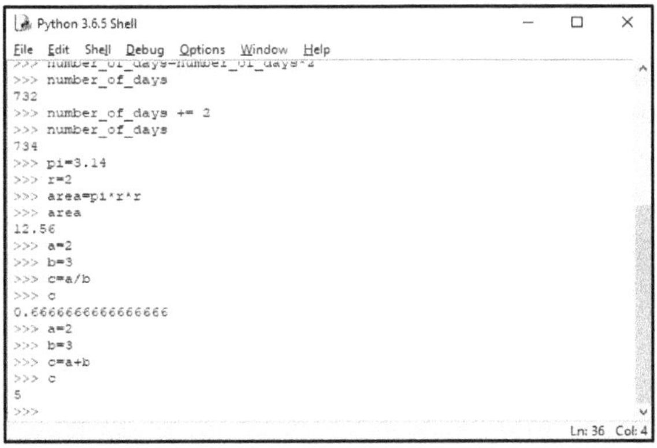

Figure 3.15. The addition operator

3.4.2. The subtraction operator: -

The usual dash sign is used as the subtraction operator:

```
a=4
b=1/4
c=a-b
```

Please note that the operation 1/4 is performed and then assigned to variable b here.

Figure 3.16. The subtraction operator

3.4.3. The multiplication operator: *

Let's calculate the number of eggs in a box in which there are 2 rows and 8 columns:

```
num_of_rows=2
num_of_columns=8
num_of_eggs=num_of_rows*num_of_columns
```

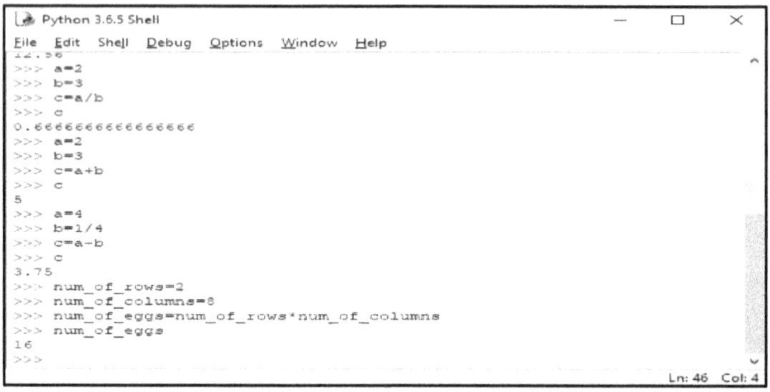

Figure 3.17. The multiplication operator

3.4.4. The division operator: /

This gives the result of the mathematical division. It is worth noting that the result of the division operator will always be as float even when both numbers around it are integers:

```
x=6/2
```

Figure 3.18. The division operator

As you can see from the output of the IDLE, the result is 3.0, not 3. There's another division operator in Python that gives integer values as explained below.

3.4.5. The floor division operator: //

This operator outputs the integer result of the division operation and neglects the fractional part of the result, if any. Let's try it as follows:

```
x=6//2
```

Figure 3.19. The floor division operator

We didn't lose any information here. But let's try a division with a fractional result:

```
x=20//6
```

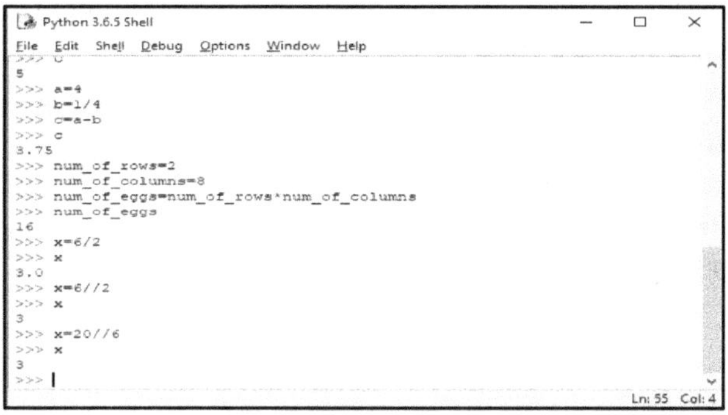

Figure 3.20. The floor division operator

The actual result of 20/6 is 3.33333333 (repeating fraction). But the fractional part is omitted here when we use the floor division operator: 20//6.

3.4.6. The modulus operator: %

This operator gives the remainder of the division operation, i.e. the modulus operation. Let's find the remainder when we divide 20 by 6:

```
x=20%6
```

Figure 3.21. The modulus operator

When we divide 20 by 6 and want an integer result, we get 3 as the result of the division and 2 as the remainder of the division.

3.4.7. The negation operator: -

This is again the dash symbol as in subtraction but used only with a single number. When we place dash in front of a number, we get the negated version of the number:

```
y=5
y=-y
```

When we send these command to Python, the variable y will have the value of -5:

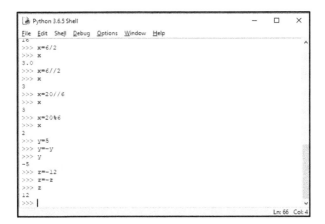

Figure 3.22. The negation of a number

We can use the same operator to convert a negative number to its positive counnterpart:

```
z=-12
z=-z
```

The variable z will have the value of +12 at the end:

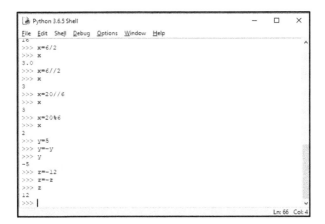

Figure 3.23. The negation of a negative number

3.4.8. The power operator: **

In mathematics, we use the the power concept to multiply a number by itself many times or to get the root of a number with the fractional powers. We can do this in Python using the ** operator. 2^3=8 as we know from maths (2^3=2*2*2=8). We can do this in Python as follows:

```
x=2**3
```

Figure 3.24. The power operator

We can also use the power operator for calculating the roots. The operation $16^{0.25}$=2 in maths (which is the same as $\sqrt[4]{16} = 16^{\frac{1}{4}}$) can be done in Python as follows: :

```
16**0.25
```

The result of this is 2.0 as expected. We can perform numerous mathematical operations by combining these operators.

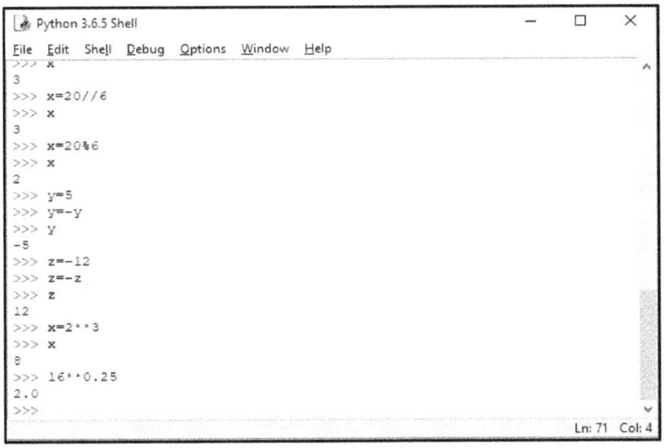

Figure 3.25. The power operator for use in calculating a root of the 4th order

Note that we didn't assign the result of the `16**0.25` operation, we used the IDLE prompt as a calculator in this case. This is because we don't need to assign the results to variables in the IDLE prompt.

3.4.9. Order of mathematical operators

When we have a long chain of mathematical operations at a single line, Python performs these operations according to the usual mathematical order, i.e. 1. The parantheses first, 2. Then the modulus and power operations, 3. Then the multiplication and division, and 3. Addition and subtraction are performed at last. Can you guess the result of the following chained operation:

```
24/2+5*2+(24+6)%3*2
```

Let's try it in IDLE as in Figure 3.26. The result is 22.0. The order is like this: firstly the operation in parantheses is perfomed: `24/2+5*2+(24+6)%3*2=24/2+5*2+30%3*2`. Then comes the modulud operator: `24/2+5*2+30%3*2=24/2+5*2+0*2`. Then the multiplication and divisions: `12.0+5*2+0`. And finally additions and subtractions: `12.0+5*2+0=22.0`. Note that the result of the division `24/2` is of float type, `12.0` therefore the overall result is also of float type.

41

```
Python 3.6.5 Shell                                    —    □    ×
File  Edit  Shell  Debug  Options  Window  Help
>>> x=20//6
>>> x
3
>>> x=20%6
>>> x
2
>>> y=5
>>> y=-y
>>> y
-5
>>> z=-12
>>> z=-z
>>> z
12
>>> x=2**3
>>> x
8
>>> 16**0.25
2.0
>>> 24/2+5*2+(24+6)%3*2
22.0
>>>
                                                          Ln: 73  Col: 4
```

Figure 3.26. A chained operation

These are the frequently used built-in standard mathematical operations. Additionally, Python has loads of free additional libraries to perform sophisticated mathematical operations such as calculus, linear algebra and numerical computations. After you grasp the basics of Python, learning to use those libraries is very easy because they all employ the same Pythonic philosophy: simple, short and effective.

Let's now study another frequently used data type in Python: strings.

3.9. String variables

Strings variables hold texts, in other words character arrays. Strings are created using single or double quotes as follows:

```
name="John"
surname='Doe'
```

We have created two string variables containing the values of *John* and *Doe*. In Python, all strings are arrays of individual characters. Therefore, the variables name and surname can also be represented as below:

name="John":

name[0]	name[1]	name[2]	name[3]
J	o	h	n

surname="Doe":

surname[0]	surname[1]	surname[2]
D	o	e

3.5.1. Accessing individual elements of a string

We can access individual elements of a string by using the appropriate indices. For example, let's access the second element (index=1) of the surname variable in IDLE:

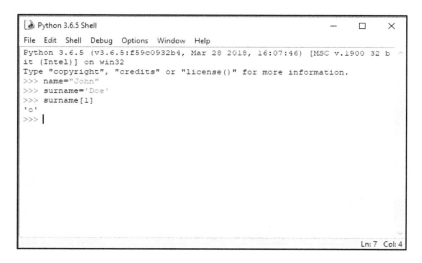

Figure 3.27. Accessing individual elements of a string

We should be careful about indexing. The indices start with 0 in Python.

We can also access the elements of a string starting from the end. For that, we will need to use negative indices:

name="John":

name[-4]	name[-3]	name[-2]	name[-1]
J	o	h	n

The last element has the index of -1 and then we can go from right to left by decreasing this number as you can see from this table. If we ask for name[-2] in Python, we get the following result as expected:

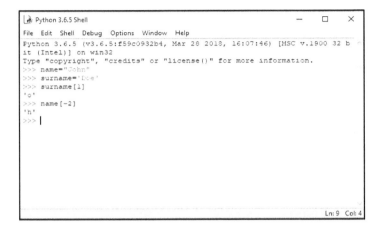

Figure 3.28. Accessing elements from the end

3.5.2. Accessing a portion of a string

We can also use the semicolon (:) operator to access more than one element of a string. The format of this command is as follows:

```
String_name[start_index: end_index: step]
```

The default value for step is 1, which means it will be taken as 1 if we do not specify it in our commands. Let's define a longer string and try to access portions of it:

```
n="Hello mate."
```

When we count the individual elements of this string, we see that it has 11 individual elements (characters):

n[0]	n[1]	n[2]	n[3]	n[4]	n[5]	n[6]	n[7]	n[8]	n[9]
H	e	l	l	o		m	a	t	e

Since the index starts at 0, the index of the final element is 10, not 11. And also note that space and the dot are also counted as individual elements and have their own indices. This is valid for any character included in strings.

Let's access the portion of this string from the second element to the fifth element:

```
n[1:5]
```

In this command, the element n[1] will included but the last element n[5] will not be included in the result. Therefore we will obtain the following portion by this command:

n[1]	n[2]	n[3]	n[4]
e	l	l	o

Let's try this in IDLE:

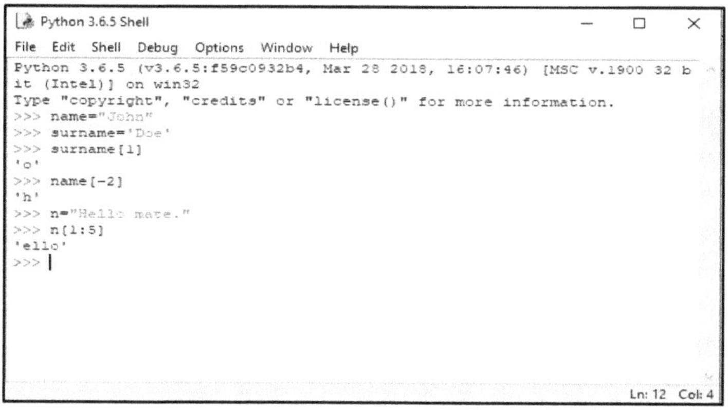

Figure 3.29. Accessing a portion of a string

If we want to access a portion starting from the beginning of the string (i.e. element with the index [0]), we can omit the first element in our command:

```
n[:5]
```

This is equivalent to:

```
n[0:5]
```

In IDLE, we get "Hello" as expected:

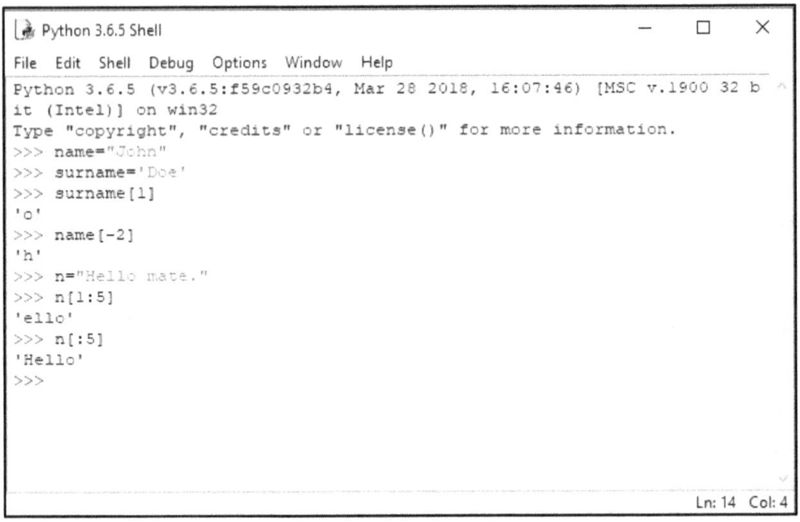

Figure 3.30. Accessing a portion of a string starting from the beginning

Similarly, if we do not specify the end_index, the portion will go from the specified starting point to the end of the string:

```
n[3:]
```

is equivalent to:

```
n[3:10]
```

Note that the number 10 is spesific to this example since it is the final index for this string. It will be different for strings with different lengths.

Let's try this in IDLE:

```
Python 3.6.5 Shell                                    —  □  ×
File Edit Shell Debug Options Window Help
Python 3.6.5 (v3.6.5:f59c0932b4, Mar 28 2018, 16:07:46) [MSC v.1900 32 b
it (Intel)] on win32
Type "copyright", "credits" or "license()" for more information.
>>> name="John"
>>> surname='Doe'
>>> surname[1]
'o'
>>> name[-2]
'h'
>>> n="Hello mate."
>>> n[1:5]
'ello'
>>> n[:5]
'Hello'
>>> n[3:]
'lo mate.'
>>> |
                                                    Ln: 16  Col: 4
```

Figure 3.31. Accessing a portion of a string starting from an index to the end

Let's now try the step option:

```
n[::2]
```

We didn't specify the start_index and end_index therefore we will access the whole string. On the other hand access one of the 2 elements in each iteration since the step option is set to 2. The result will have the following elements:

n[0]	n[2]	n[4]	n[6]	n[8]	n[10]
H	l	o	m	t	.

You can see the result in IDLE in Figure 3.32.

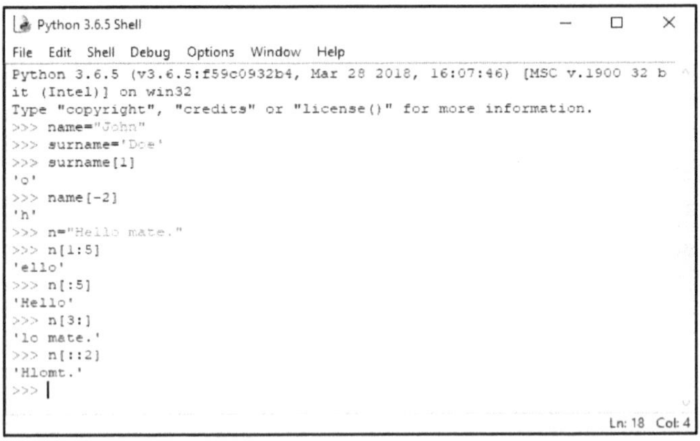

Figure 3.32. Using the step option when accessing a portion of a string

Let's use all the options of the command. Can yuu guess the result when the following line is executed in IDLE:

```
n[3:10:3]
```

It says: "Start from the element with index 3 and go to the element with index 10 (not included) and take 1 in 3 elements on your way". Therefore the result will have the following elements: n[3], n[6], n[9]:

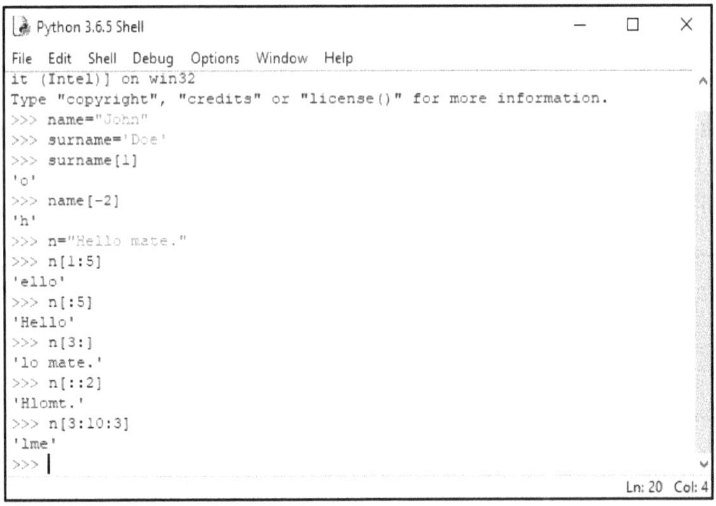

Figure 3.33. Using all the options in the string portioning command

Let's now try someting more complicated:

```
n[-2::-2]
```

The starting index is -2 meaning the element just before the last element: "e". The step option is -2 meaning that we will move from right to left and get 1 of 2 elements on our way. The end_index is not given so we will sweep all the elements from to the beginning of the string:

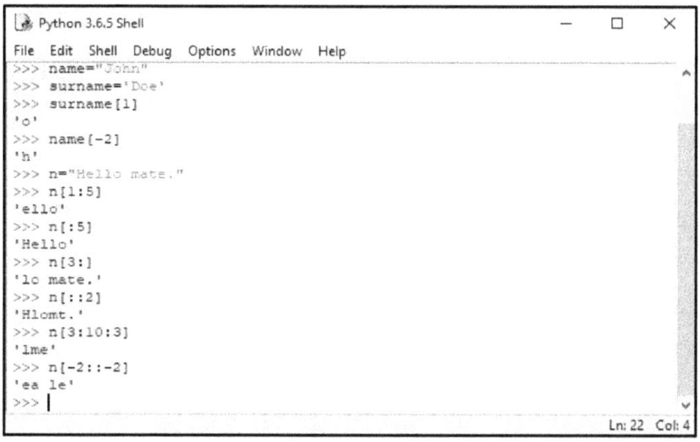

Figure 3.34. The result of the command n[-2::-2]

We can also invert the string by going from right to left with the step option as -1:

```
n[::-1]
```

Figure 3.35. Inverting the string by n[::-1]

3.5.3. Finding the length of a string

There's a frequently used function for strings in Python: the len() function. It returns (gives) the length of the string given as an argument. Let's find the length of our string n:

```
len(n)
```

Python gives 11 as expected:

Figure 3.36. Using the len() function for strings

3.5.4. String concatenation

We can also concatenate (add) strings using the addition operator (+) in Python:

```
f="first"
s="second"
t="third"
c=f+s+t
```

The last command will add the three strings as shown in Figure 3.37.

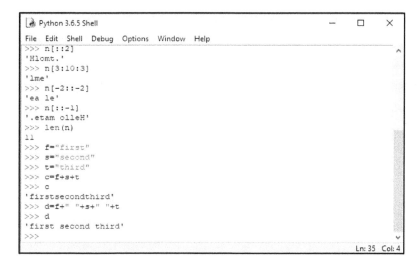

Figure 3.37. Concatenating strings

We can also add spaces during concatenation, we just need to add strings made of a single spaces in between:

```
d=f+" "+s+" "+t
```

Figure 3.38. Adding spaces between strings

Note: Be careful not to forget the spaces inside the space strings. I mean if we just write "", this is not a space. We need to use " ".

We can also use the multiplication operator with strings. It multiplies the string (literally, the Pythonic way!):

```
3*f
```

The result is 3*"first"="firstfirstfirst":

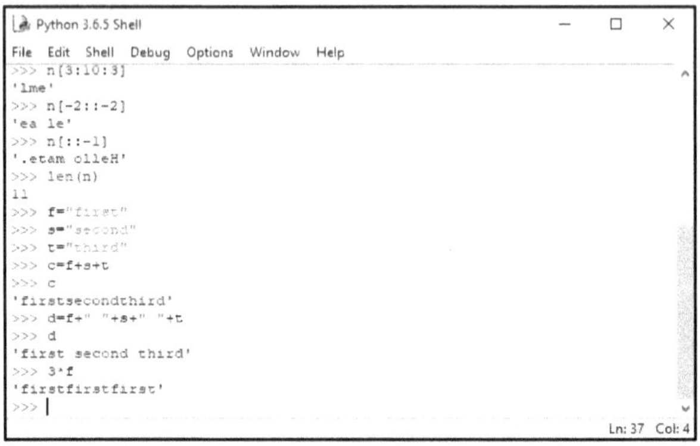

Figure 3.39. Multiplication of a string

We can combine the addition and multiplication operations too:

```
2*f+s+3*t
```

The result is "firstfirstsecondthirdthirdthird" as shown in Figure 3.40.

Figure 3.40. Using the addition and multiplication operators together

3.6. Converting strings to numbers and vice versa

We usually need to convert strings to numbers (integers or floats) because when a user enters data into the Python, it is taken as a string and if we need to do maths on it, we need to convert this data to a number type.

We can use the `int()` function for converting a string to an integer. We will give the string as the argument to the function and it will return an integer. For example:

```
a="356"
type(a)
b=int(a)
type(b)
b
```

We have defined a to be "356". Note that since we have quotation marks around it, this variable is created as a string and not an integer. We checked its type in the second line. Then, we have created a new variable, b and assigned the result of the `int(a)` function to it. `int(a)` converted the string a to an integer. We then checked its type and asked for its value:

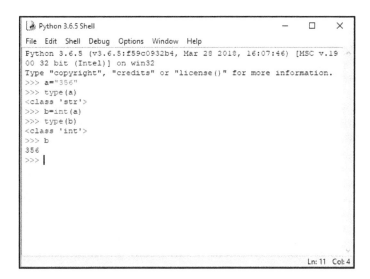

Figure 3.41. Converting a string to an integer

Note that the contents of the string has to be suitable for converting to an integer. If it is not, then Python will not do the conversion and issue an error written in red. Let's try to convert unsitable strings to integers using the int() function:

```
c=int("3.4")
d=int("Hello")
```

The string at the first line has a floating point hence cannot be converted to an integer. And the string at the second line is just non-numerical characters and also not suitable for integer conversion:

```
Python 3.6.5 Shell                                    —    □    ×
File  Edit  Shell  Debug  Options  Window  Help
00 32 bit (Intel)] on win32
Type "copyright", "credits" or "license()" for more information.
>>> a="356"
>>> type(a)
<class 'str'>
>>> b=int(a)
>>> type(b)
<class 'int'>
>>> b
356
>>> c=int("3.4")
Traceback (most recent call last):
  File "<pyshell#5>", line 1, in <module>
    c=int("3.4")
ValueError: invalid literal for int() with base 10: '3.4'
>>> d=int("Hello")
Traceback (most recent call last):
  File "<pyshell#6>", line 1, in <module>
    d=int("Hello")
ValueError: invalid literal for int() with base 10: 'Hello'
>>>
                                                    Ln: 21  Col: 4
```

Figure 3.42. Trying to convert unsuitable strings to integers

We can also convert float type variables to strings. We use the float() function for this:

```
pi_string=float("3.14")
```

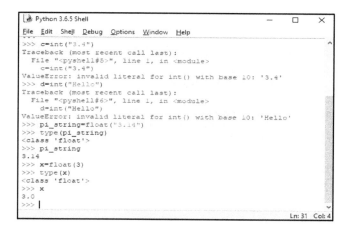

Figure 3.43. Converting float to string using the `float()` function

The `int()` function gave error when we tried to convert a float-like string above. Let's try the opposite: giving an integer-like string to the `float()` function:

```
x=float("3")
type(x)
x
```

Python successfully converts the integer-like string to a float type:

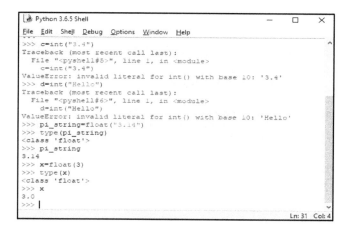

Figure 3.44. Converting an integer-like string to float using the `float()` function

55

We converted strings to numbers. Can we convert integers and floats to string? Absolutely, with a single simple function: str():

```
i=4
f=4.5
str(i)
str(f)
```

The results of these operations are given in Figure 3.45. Please note the quotes around the results which mean that these are strings.

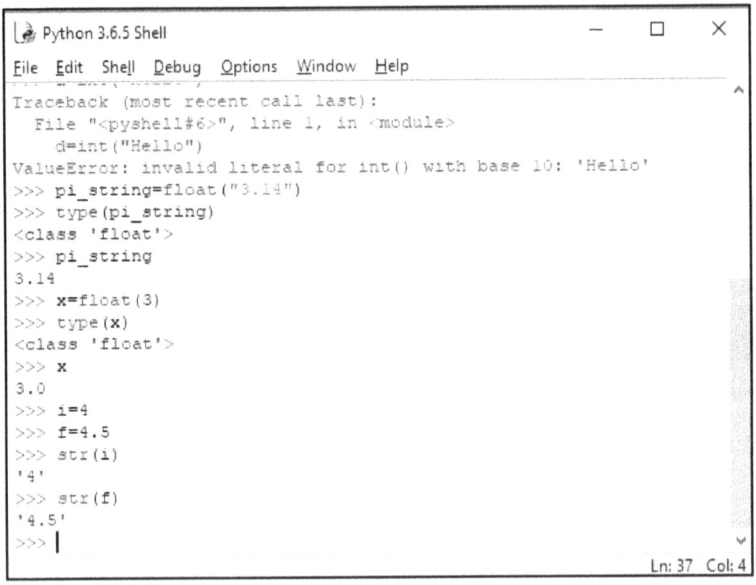

Figure 3.45. Converting integer and float to string

By the way, we can also convert integers and floats to each other using the int() and float() functions, but this is rarely used:

```
a=float(3)
type(a)
a
b=int(3.14)
type(b)
b
```

The results are shown in Figure 3.46. Please note that the int() function just neglects the fractional part of the float variable given to it therefore we lose information with this conversion.

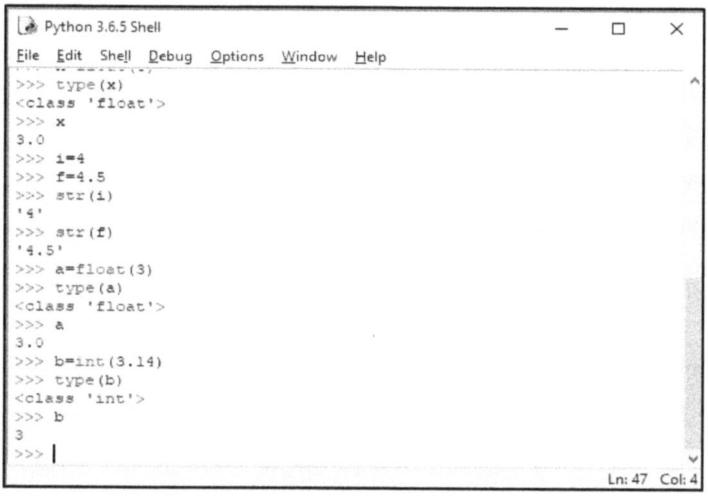

Figure 3.46. Converting an integer to float and vice versa

3.7. The *print()* function and output formatting

We have just written the names of the variables to ask for its contents in the IDLE prompt. This OK if we are using the IDLE prompt as a live interface for communicationg with Python. But as you may have noticed, we lose our commands when we restart the IDLE and we cannot share these commands. In order to save our Python programs, we need to write our commands to a text file with an extension .py. We can do this in IDLE. Just navigate to File in the top menu and click the New File button as shown in Figure 3.47.

A new empty Python source file will be created and opened in the Editor as in Figure 3.48.

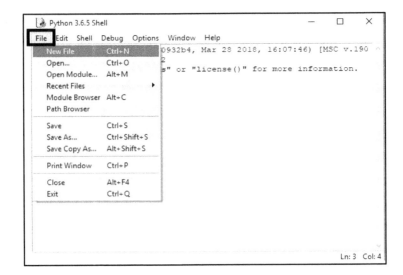

Figure 3.47. Opening a new file in IDLE

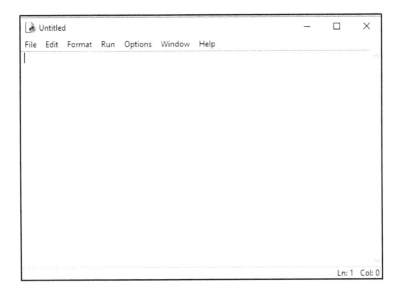

Figure 3.48. The Editor

We can write our commands in this file and save it for later use, share it or run it. As an example, let's define an integer, increment it by 2 and convert it to a string:

```
a=4
a += 2
b=str(a)
b
```

We will write this program on the Editor and save it somewhere on our computer (just use File-->Save button to save it as usual) as shown in Figure 3.49. I named it as python_program_3_1.py and saved it to my Desktop. We were entering commands one by one in the IDLE prompt but in the Editor, we enter all commands ate once. However, when we run this program, Python will execute each statement from top to down again one by one.

It is also eay to run our program saved in the file. Just go to Run from the top menu and then select Run Module button as shown in Figure 3.50. As you can see from the button, you can also run the program by pressing F5 on your keyboard. OK, let's do it, click the Run Module button and see what will appear in the IDLE prompt (the outputs of our program are displayed again in the IDLE prompt).

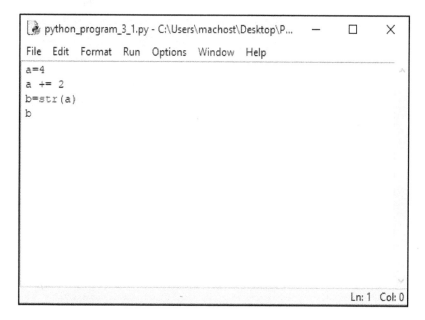

Figure 3.49. Our program written in the Editor and saved to a file

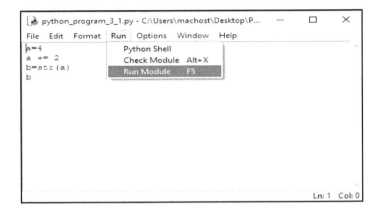

Figure 3.50. Running our first program

The output after running our program is displayed in Figure 3.51. According to our knowledge from before, our program listing will create a as 4 and then increment it by 2, making a=6, and then create a string variable b which will be "6". These are OK. But the last line where we have written the name of the string variable b didn't give any output in the IDLE. IDLE prompt only notified us that our python_program_1.py was executed. *We know that if we executed these command in the IDLE prompt, it would output the content of the variable b. But this is not the case in saved programs (for programs sent to Python and not entered to the IDLE prompt).*

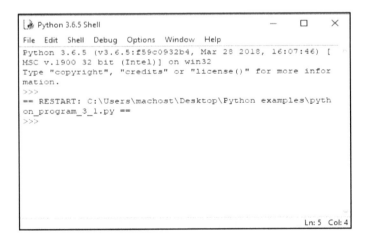

Figure 3.51. The IDLE prompt after we run our program

So, how can we output the contents of variables in our Python programs? We simply use the print() function. Let's modify our program to use this function for displaying the contents of variable b:

```
a=4
a += 2
b=str(a)
print(b)
```

I have saved the program as python_program_3_2.py and run it. The Python output at the IDLE prompt is as shown in Figure 3.52. The print(b) line printed the current value of variable b. We can print the values of integers and floats too using the print() function.

We can use more than one argument inside the print() function. It would be more meaningful to output the value of b as b=6. We can use the print() function in the following way for this:

```
a=4
a += 2
b=str(a)
print("b=",b)
```

We sent two arguments inside the print() function here. Output of this program is shown in Figure 3.53.

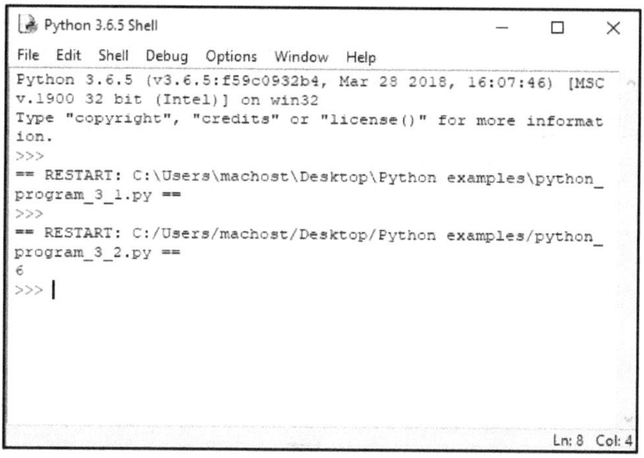

Figure 3.52. Python output of python_program_3_2.py

```
Python 3.6.5 Shell                                    —    □    ×
File  Edit  Shell  Debug  Options  Window  Help
Python 3.6.5 (v3.6.5:f59c0932b4, Mar 28 2018, 16:07:46) [MSC
v.1900 32 bit (Intel)] on win32
Type "copyright", "credits" or "license()" for more informat
ion.
>>>
== RESTART: C:\Users\machost\Desktop\Python examples\python_
program_3_1.py ==
>>>
== RESTART: C:/Users/machost/Desktop/Python examples/python_
program_3_2.py ==
6
>>>
== RESTART: C:/Users/machost/Desktop/Python examples/python_
program_3_3.py ==
b= 6
>>> |
                                                     Ln: 11   Col: 4
```

Figure 3.52. Python output of python_program_3_3.py

We can format string variables for printing in a formatted way. We use special characters for this aim. For example, if we want to print two strings in different lines, we can use \n operator (newline operator) as follows:

```
s1="Hello"
s2="mate"
print(s1, "\n", s2)
```

Note that the spaces between the arguments of functions are optional. Let's write these as a program and try in Python:

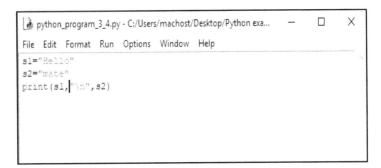

Figure 3.54. Formatting output

The result is as expected:

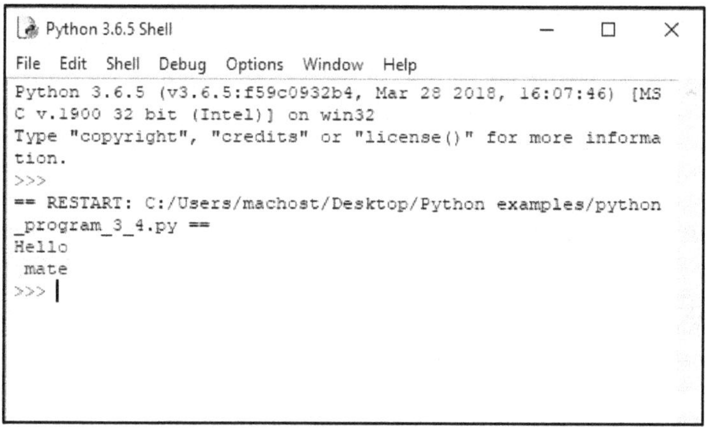

Figure 3.55. Formatted output with \n

Another widely used operator for formatting the output is \t. It places a tab (8 spaces) between the arguments of the print function:

```
s1="Hello"
s2="mate"
print(s1,"\t",s2)
```

Its output is as follows:

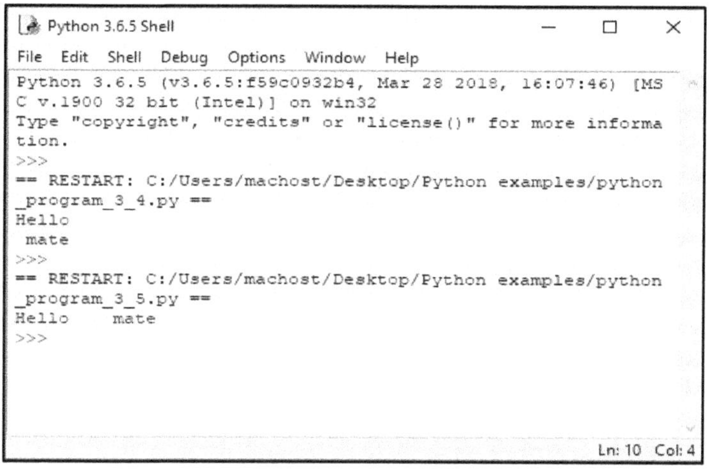

Figure 3.56. Formatted output with \t

We can also use seperators in the print() function. We just need to specify the seperator character using the sep keyword:

```
s1="Hello"
s2="mate"
print(s1,s2, sep="-")
```

The output is s1 and s2 strings with the seperator (dash) between them as shown in Figure 3.57. Please note that the default value for the seperator is blank if not specified. We can use any string as the seperator.

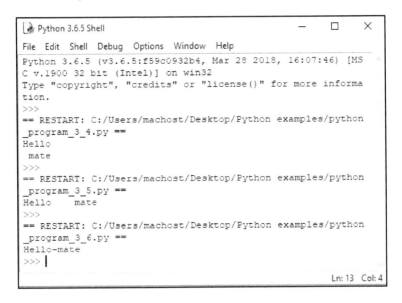

Figure 3.57. Using a seperator with the print() function

Another operator used in conjunction with the print() function is the * seperator. When we place a * in front of a string, it commands the print() function to print each character of the string seperately. For example:

```
print(*"I love programming!")
```

This line will output each character seperated by spaces (remember that the default seperator for the print() is space.):

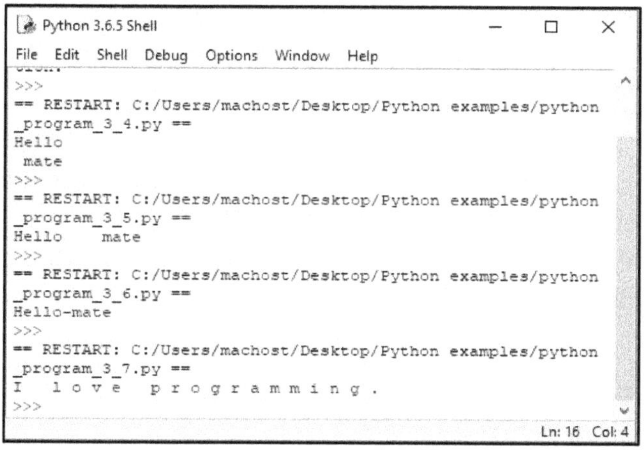

Figure 3.58. Using the * operator to split a string in `print()` function

We can use a different seperator too. For example, let's split the same string with newline ("\n") so that each character in the string will be printed in a new line:

```
print(*"I love programming!", sep="\n")
```

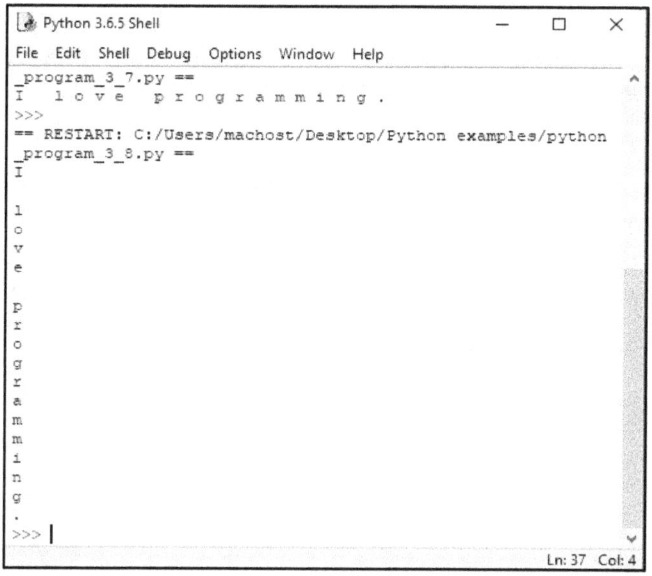

Figure 3.59. Splitting a string with a newline seperator

We sometimes need to insert a multiple variable values inside a string. We use a method named `format()` for this aim. Methods are similar to functions but the main difference from the application viewpoint is that methods are applied to objects while functions are executed independently. We will apply the `format()` method to a string object for inserting values to the string. Better to see this on an example. Let's set the radius of a circle to be 2 and calculate its area. And then print both the radius and the area in the same line by inserting these values inside the string:

```
radius=2
pi=3.14
area=pi*radius**2
print("The area of the circle having {} of radius
is {}".format(radius, area))
```

Note that our string to be printed is `"The area of the circle having {} of radius is {}"`. We inserted curly brackets at the places where we want to insert the values of the `radius` and `area` variables. Then we apply the `format()` method with the dot operator to the string (shown as underlined above for taking your attention but it won't be underlined in the Python file). The arguments to the `format()` method are the variables to be inserted at the places held by the curly brackets. With the above expression, the `format()` method will insert the value of the `radius` variable at the place of the first curly bracket while the second bracket's place will be populated by the value of the `area` variable.

Let's run this program in Python (python_program_3_9.py) to see its formatted output as in Figure 3.60.

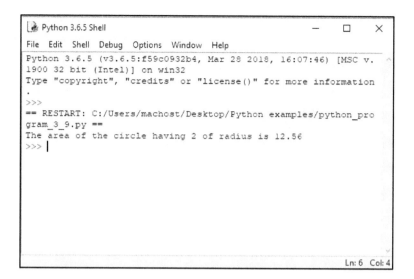

Figure 3.60. The formatted output using the format() method

3.8. Accepting input from the user-the *input()* function

We have assigned the values of the variables inside our program until now. However, we obviously need to get input from the user so that our program will have meaningful applications. We simply use the `input()` function for this aim. Let's modify the area example above to take the value of the radius from the user. The argument of the input function is the string to be displayed to the user:

```
radius=float(input("Please enter the radius of the circle: "))
pi=3.14
area=pi*radius**2
print("The area of the circle having {} of radius is {}".format(radius, area))
```

Note that the output of the `input()` function is string type therefore we need to convert it to int or float if we will do maths on it. Therefore we used the `float()` function chained to the `input()` function here.

When we execute this Python file, the IDLE prompt will ask for an input as follows:

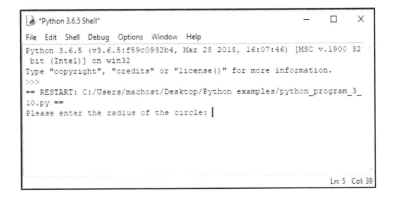

Figure 3.61. IDLE prompt asking for input

We can enter any value here, I entered 2 and the output of the program is dieplayed instantly:

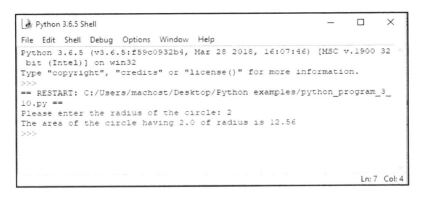

Figure 3.62. The output of our program

The most important point we need to be aware of is using the appropriate type conversions by the `input()` function.

We have learned primitive variable types until here. Now, it's time to see special variable types available in Python.

3.9. Lists in python

Lists are used to hold related (or consecutive) data in Python. For example, we can hold the integers from 1 to 5 in 5 different integers but this wouldn't be practical. We can store these values in a list type which has 10 cells as follows:

Index: 0	Index: 1	Index: 2	Index: 3	Index: 4
Value:1	Value:2	Value:3	Value:4	Value:5

Structures of lists are similar to those of strings. In strings, we stored character data in each cell but in lists, we can store any variable type. Lists are defined using square brackets.

Let's create a list in Python with numbers from 1 to 10 and print the value of the element havng the index of 4:

```
my_list=[1,2,3,4,5,6,7,8,9,10]
print(my_list[4])
```

```
Python 3.6.5 Shell                               —    □    ✕
File  Edit  Shell  Debug  Options  Window  Help
Python 3.6.5 (v3.6.5:f59c0932b4, Mar 28 2018, 16:07:46) [MSC v.
1900 32 bit (Intel)] on win32
Type "copyright", "credits" or "license()" for more information
.
>>>
== RESTART: C:/Users/machost/Desktop/Python examples/python_pro
gram_3_11.py ==
5
>>> |
                                                 Ln: 6  Col: 4
```

Figure 3.63. The 5th element (index:4) in our list

We can also create a list with different types of variables inside:

```
list1=[1, 1.5, "Hello"]
```

And also use the `len()` function to obtain the number of elements:

```
print("Number of elements in list1: ", len(list1))
```

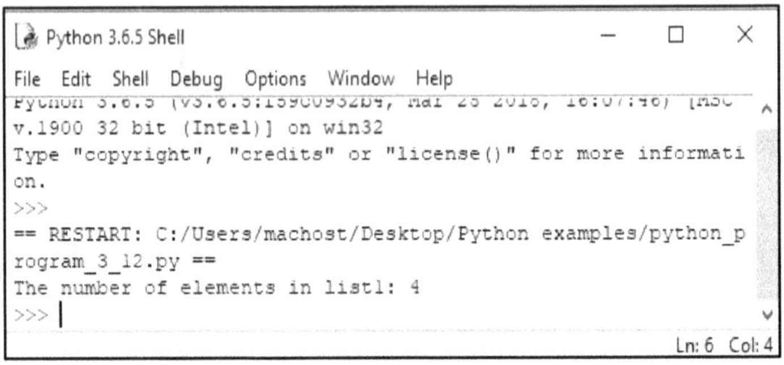

Figure 3.64. Getting the number of elements in a list

We can also convert a string to a list of characters using the `list()` function as follows:

```
str1="Python"
list1=list(str1)
print(list1)
```

Let's see the format of the output of the `print()` function in the above code:

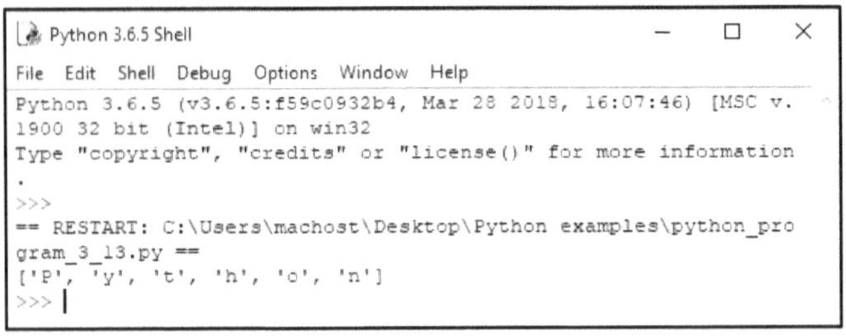

Figure 3.65. The format of the printed list

As we can see from this output, each character in the string is assigned as a new element in the list.

We can also create an empty list for adding elements later with the list() function:

```
Python 3.6.5 Shell                                    —    □    ×
File  Edit  Shell  Debug  Options  Window  Help
Python 3.6.5 (v3.6.5:f59c0932b4, Mar 28 2018, 16:07:46) [MSC
v.1900 32 bit (Intel)] on win32
Type "copyright", "credits" or "license()" for more informati
on.
>>>
== RESTART: C:/Users/machost/Desktop/Python examples/python_p
rogram_3_14.py ==
[]
>>> |
                                                        Ln: 6  Col: 4
```

Figure 3.66. An empty list printed at the prompt

We have seen indexing and splitting of strings before. These operations are similar in lists. We access each element in the list using the index in square brackets as we have done above. We can also split a list with the following template:

```
list[start_index:stop_index:step]
```

If we do not specify the step parameter, it will have the default value of 1 as in strings. Another similarity is that the stop_index is excluded. Let's define a new list and do some splitting operations:

```
list1=[1,2,4.5,"Air", 4/5, 22]

print("list1[2:4]:", list1[2:4])
print("list1[:3:2]:", list1[:3:2])
print("list1[::-1]:", list1[::-1])
```

The first operation takes the elements with indices 2 (element: 4.5) and 3 (element: "Air"), element with index 4 is not included. The second operation did not specify the beginning index therefore it will start from the beginning of the list and sweep until element with index 3 (again not included). However it will take 1 of 2 elements during the sweep as the step parameter is set as 2. Therefore it will take the elements with indices 0 and 2 only. And the third operation will sweep the list from start to the end because no beginning ot ending şndex is given. However the step is -1 meaning that the operation will sweep from the last element to the first element of the list. Let's see these operations in IDLE by executing the above program:

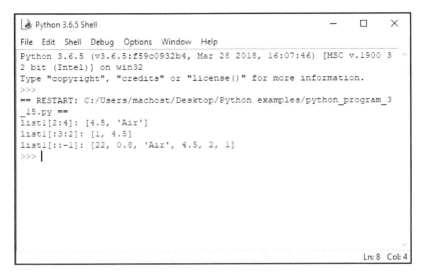

Figure 4.67. Various splitting operations on a list

3.9.1. Various operations on lists

We can change the individual elements of the list by assigning a new value as follows:

```
list2=[3.14, 34, "Air", 45]
list2[1]=200
print(list2)
```

We just changed the second element (which has the index of 1):

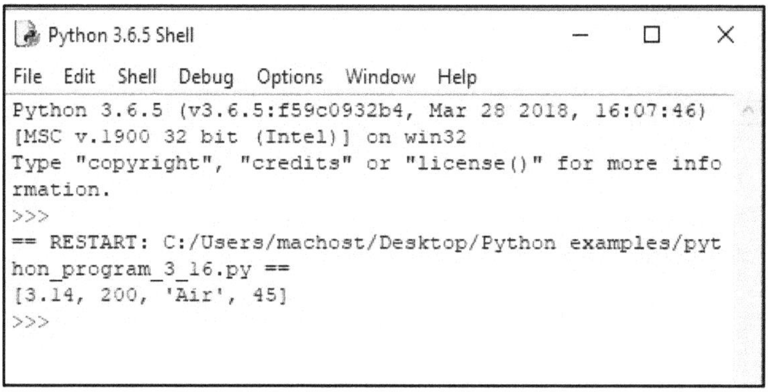

Figure 4.68. Changing an individual element of a list

We can also add lists or multiply lists by a number as we did in strings:

```
list2=[3.14, 34, "Air", 45]
print(2*list2)
print(list2+[23, "a"])
```

The list is multiplied by 2 in the first operation hence its structure is repeated twice, and in the second operation list2 and the list [23, "a"] will be merged in order as can be seen below:

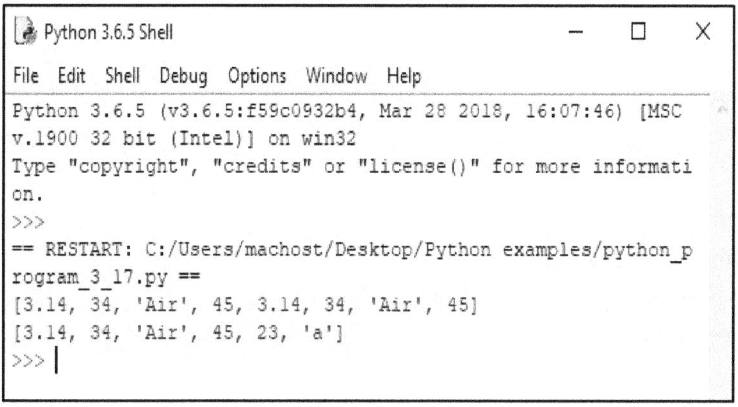

Figure 4.69. List multiplication and addition examples

There are also several methods those can be applied on lists to alter their elements. One of them is the append() method. Append method adds elements at the end of the list:

```
list_name.append(element to be inserted)
```

We have created list2 above as list2=[3.14, 34, "Air", 45]. Let's add another element to the end of this list:

```
list2=[3.14, 34, "Air", 45]
list2.append(12.7)
print(list2)
```

We have added the new element to the list as shown below:

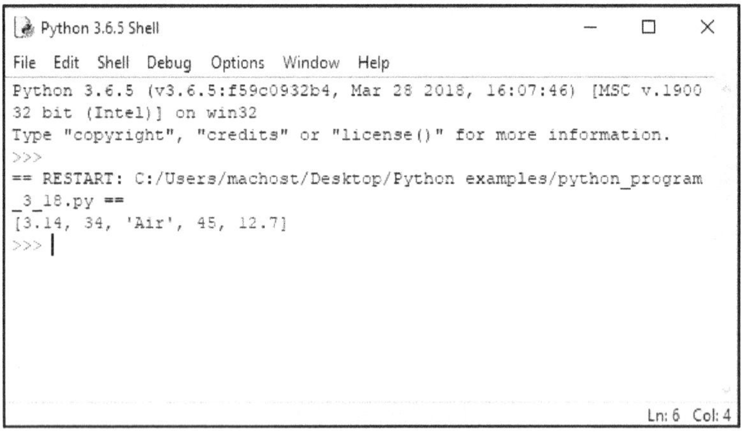

Figure 4.70. A new element is appended to list2

Another useful method is the pop() method. When the method has no arguments, it pops, i.e. removes, the last element of the list it is applied to. Alternatively, if an index is given as an argument to it, it removes the corresponding element. Let's apply the pop() method to list2 without any argument first:

```
list2=[3.14, 34, "Air", 45]
list2.pop()
print(list2)
```

The last element, 45, is removed from `list2` after the `pop()` method is applied:

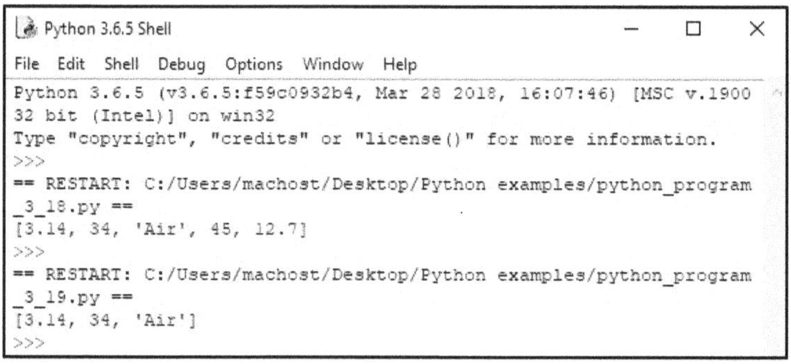

Figure 4.71. Using the pop() method without an argument

Let's try the same example by specifying index:1 as the argument to the `pop()` method:

```
list2=[3.14, 34, "Air", 45]
list2.pop(1)
print(list2)
```

In this case, the element with index:1, which is 34, will be removed from the list:

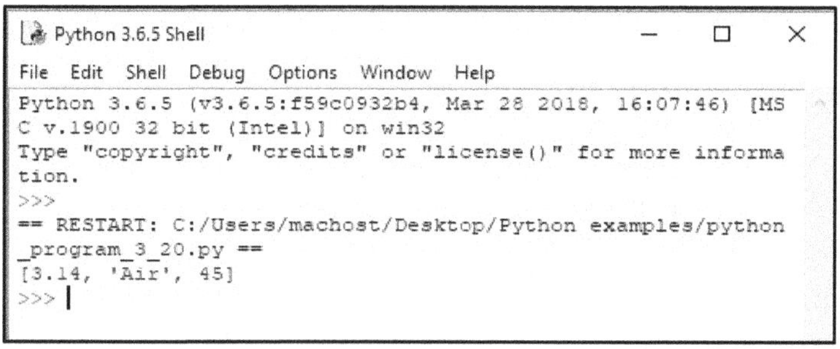

Figure 4.72. Contents of list2 after applying the pop() method with the argument of 1

The last method we will consider for lists is the sort() method. It sorts the elements of the list if the list has the same type of elements. *The elements of the list will be sorted and the sorted form will be stored in the same list.* If the elements are of numeric type, it will sort from smaller to greater element. If the elements are of string type, it will sort alphabetically:

```
list3=[4,6,1,9,8]
list4=["Python", "C", "C++", "Java", "Swift"]
list3.sort()
list4.sort()
print("Sorted form of list3 is", list3)
print("Sorted form of list4 is", list4)
```

Let's see the sorted forms of these lists:

```
Python 3.6.5 Shell                                    —    □    ✕

File  Edit  Shell  Debug  Options  Window  Help
Python 3.6.5 (v3.6.5:f59c0932b4, Mar 28 2018, 16:07:46) [MSC v.190
0 32 bit (Intel)] on win32
Type "copyright", "credits" or "license()" for more information.
>>>
== RESTART: C:/Users/machost/Desktop/Python examples/python_progra
m_3_21.py ==
Sorted form of list3 is [1, 4, 6, 8, 9]
Sorted form of list4 is ['C', 'C++', 'Java', 'Python', 'Swift']
>>>

                                                        Ln: 7  Col: 4
```

Figure 3.73. Sorted lists

We can also reverse the order of sorting if we set the reverse parameter of the sort() method as True. *The keyword True here is a logical variable whih can either be True or False and nothing else.* The default value of the reverse parameter is False in the sort method (it means if we do not specify any argument in the sort() method, the reverse parameter is taken as False meaning logic 0 or negative). Let's set the reverse parameters as True in the above example:

```
list3=[4,6,1,9,8]
list4=["Python", "C", "C++", "Java", "Swift"]
list3.sort(reverse=True)
list4.sort(reverse=True)
print("Sorted form of list3 is", list3)
print("Sorted form of list4 is", list4)
```

The lists will be sorted in decreasing order now:

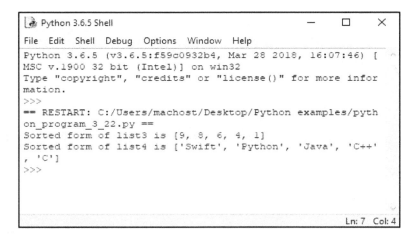

Figure 3.74. Lists sorted in reverse order

3.9.2. 2-dimensional lists

We can also create list of lists, which are called as 2-dimensional (2D) lists as follows:

```
list2D=[[4, 5, 7], [10, "Air", 4.5], [1, 6, 90]]
```

We access the elements of 2D lists by first accessing the corresponding inside list and then accessing its element as usual. Let's access the first element of list2D:

```
list2D[0]
```

This will output the first element of our main list: [4,5,7]. We then further access the elements inside this one by indexing again. Let's access the second element (which hads the value of 5):

```
list2D[0][1]
```

We access to individual elements of a 2D list by considering it as a shell as above. Let's try these in our program:

```
list2D=[[4, 5, 7], [10, "Air", 4.5], [1, 6, 90]]
print("list2D[0] is:", list2D[0])
print("list2D[0][1] is:", list2D[0][1])
```

The output in Python is as follows:

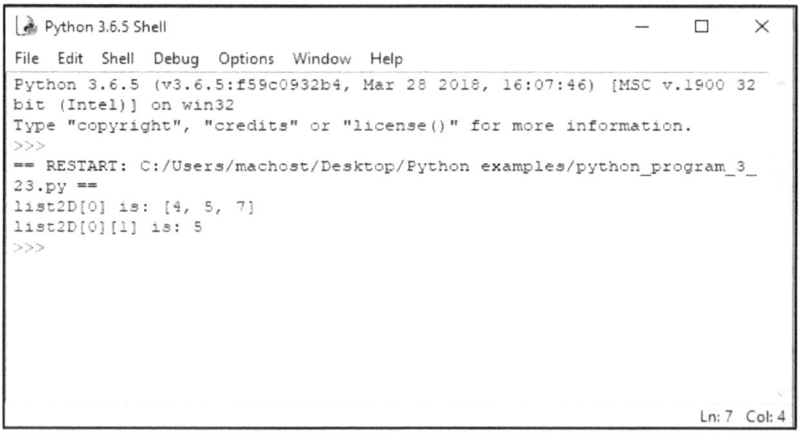

Figure 3.75. Accessing the elements of a 2D list

The functions and methods related to 1D lists are valid also for 2D lists.

We have seen that properties and accessing elements of strings and lists are very similar. However, there's an important difference: changing individual elements. We can't change individual characters in a string. If we try the following code in Python, we get an error:

```
string1="Python"
string1[0]="C"
```

We try to assign a new value "C" to the first character of the string here and we get the following error:

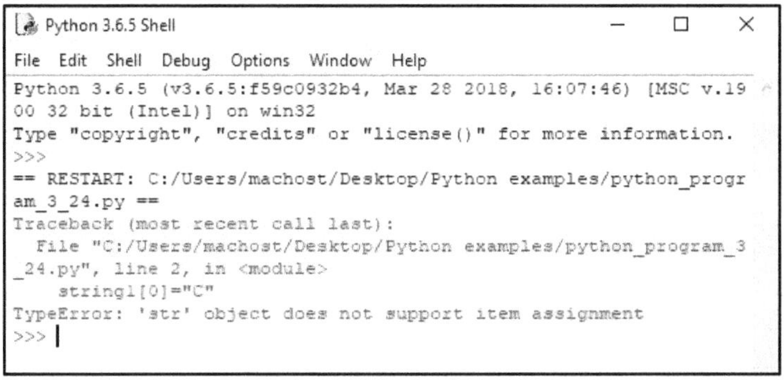

Figure 3.76. Error of assigning a new value to an individual element of a string

Python says that string object does not support item assignment. On the other hand, modifying individual elements of a list is supported:

```
list1=[24, "Air", 32.5]
list1[1]=100
print("list1: ", list1)
```

The second element of list1 (element "Air") is modified as 100 in this program:

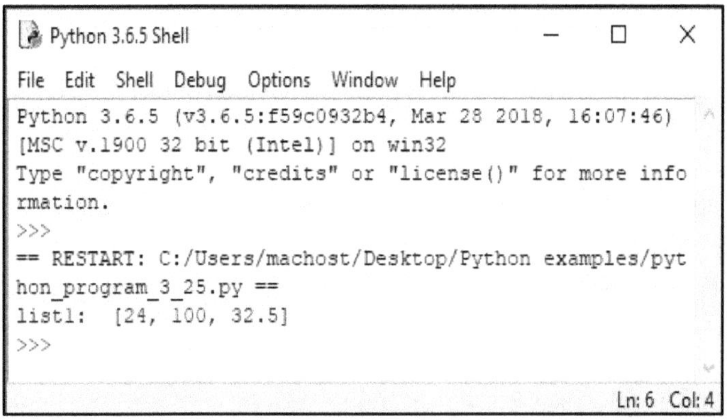

Figure 3.77. Changing the individual element of a list

3.10. Boolean variables

Since we used Boolean parameters in the sort() method of lists, I'd like to give a bit more information on Boolean variables in Python. Boolean (logical) variables are the variables which can only take one of the two possible values: True or False. The True and False are special keyword reserved for this purpose in Python. Let's see these variables in an example:

```
logical_var=True
logical_var
logical_var = not logical_var
logical_var
```

In this program we created a boolean variable called logical_var and then printed its contents. And then we used the *not operator* on this variable which toggles its value between True and False. And then we again printed its contents in the IDLE prompt. Let's see its output:

```
Python 3.6.5 Shell                                        —    □    ✕
File  Edit  Shell  Debug  Options  Window  Help
Python 3.6.5 (v3.6.5:f59c0932b4, Mar 28 2018, 16:07:46) [MSC v.
1900 32 bit (Intel)] on win32
Type "copyright", "credits" or "license()" for more information
.
>>>
 RESTART: C:/Users/machost/Desktop/Python examples/python_progr
am_3_boolean.py
Value: True
New value: False
>>> |
                                                         Ln: 7  Col: 4
```

Figure 3.78. Using Boolean variables

3.11. Tuples in Python

Tuples are similar to lists, i.e. they store values in the cells of a single variable however, their main difference is that values of individual elements of tuples cannot be changed. We define tuples using parantheses:

```
my_tuple=(3, 5, 8, 4, 3. 6)
another_tuple=(2,)
```

Note that a tuple with a single element is defined as in the second line above.

We can access the elements of a tuple using indices as we did in lists:

```
print(my_tuple[2])    # Prints the third element
(index: 2) of the tuple
print(my_tuple[:2])  #Prints the elements with
indices from 0 to 2 (not included)
print(my_tuple[-1]) # Prints the last element of
the tuple
```

We have used *comments* in the above code segment. These are the informative text that start with a hash # symbol. Python ignores the text written after the hash symbol, these are the text which are used to give information to people reading our code.

Let's try these code segmets in Python:

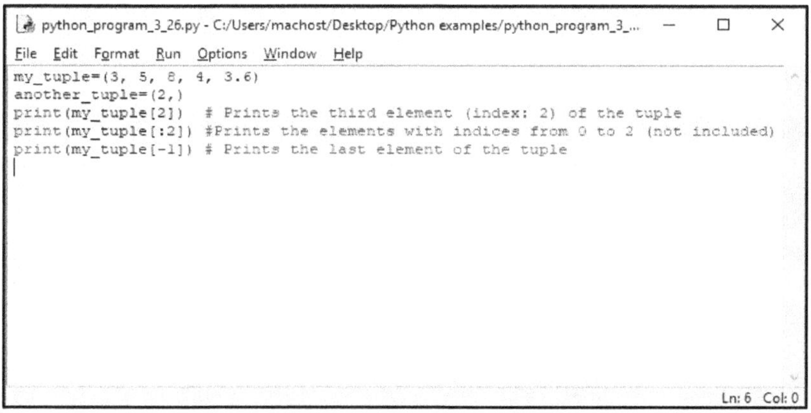

Figure 3.79. Using tuples in Python

Note that the comment text are coloured as red by the IDLE editor. (Remember that you can view the colour versions of the figures of this book at the book's companion website www.yamaclis.com/python)

Let's see the output:

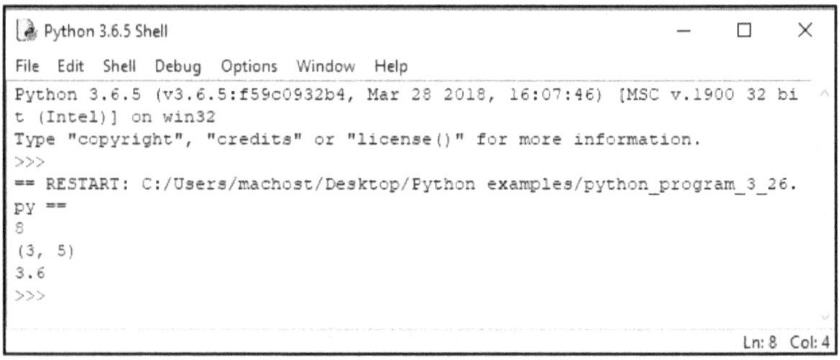

Figure 3.80. Output of example using tuples

There are some methods special for tuples. For example, the count() method returns the number of repetitions of an element in a tuple:

```python
new_tuple=(3,4,7,8,3,8,"Hello", 4.5, "Hello")
print("Number of the repetitions of 3:",
new_tuple.count(3))
print("Number of the repetitions of "Hello":",
new_tuple.count("Hello"))
```

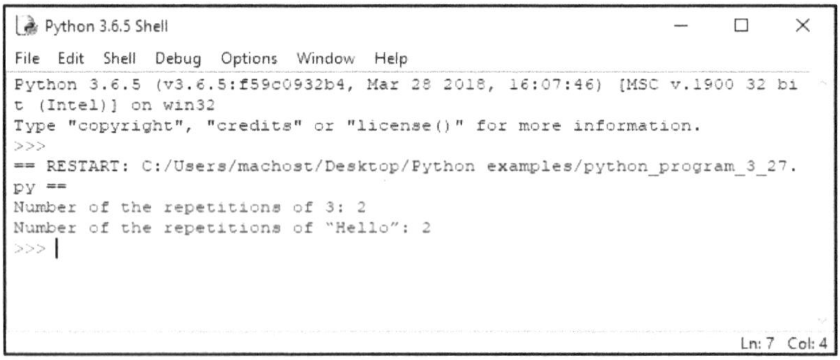

Figure 3.81. Finding number of repetitions in a tuple

Another frequently used method is the index() method which returns the index of an element in the tuple. The argument to this function is the element to be asked:

```python
new_tuple=(3,4,7,8,3,8,"Hello", 4.5, "Hello")
print("The element 7 is at the index:",
new_tuple.index(7))
```

The output says that 7 is at index 2 (3rd element in the tuple):

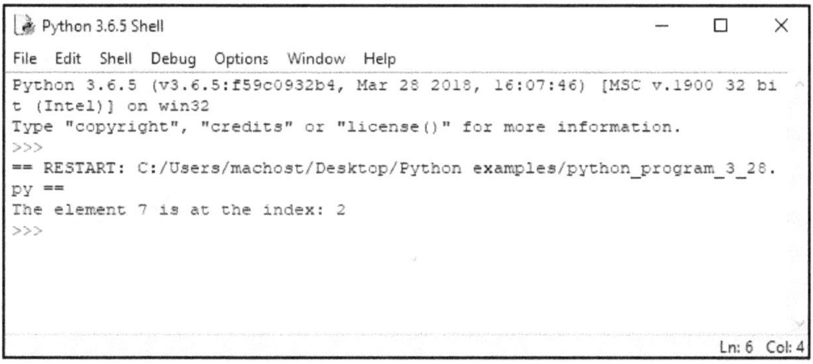

Figure 3.82. Using the index method on a tuple

What if we ask the index of a repeating element?

```
new_tuple=(3,4,7,8,3,8,"Hello", 4.5, "Hello")
print("The element 3 is at the index:",
new_tuple.index(3))
```

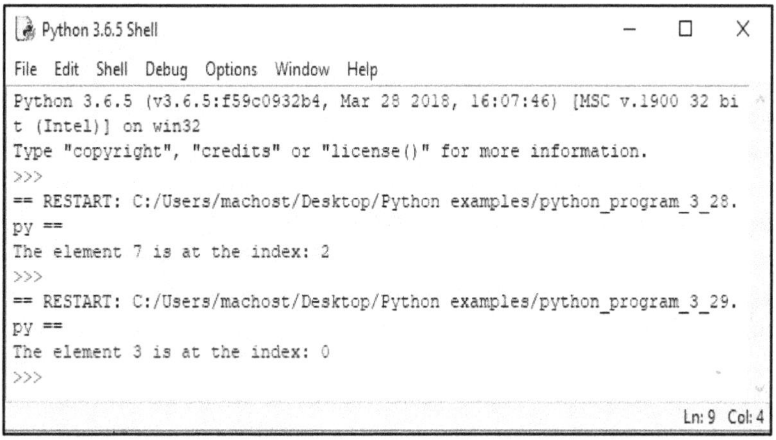

Figure 3.83. Asking the index of a repeating element

Python returns the index of the first occurence of the element as you can see above.

We have said that we cannot change the individual elements of tuples as in strings. Let's try to modify (reassign) a single element in the tuple:

```
new_tuple=(3,4,7,8,3,8,"Hello", 4.5, "Hello")
new_tuple[4]=5 # Incorrect operation. Will issue an
error.
```

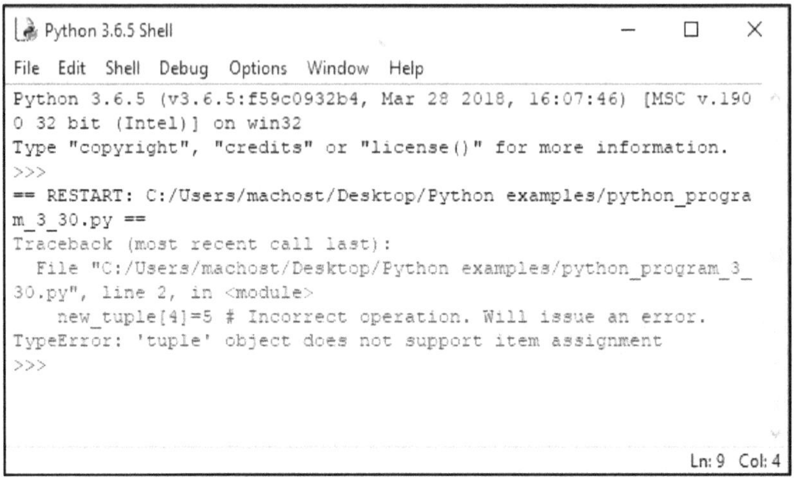

Figure 3.84. Item reassignment is not permitted in Python

Since the elements of tuples are unchangeable, they are used in the situations where we need to define constants in a program.

3.12. Dictionaries in Python

These are the data structures in which the values are indexed by a key not by an index as in the dictionaries we use in spoken languages. Dictionaries are created by using the curly brackets in Python an each key:value pair is sperated by a comma as in lists and tuples:

```
my_dict={"quince":"yellow", "strawberry":"red",
"grape":"green"}
print("The value of the key: strawberry is:",
my_dict["strawberry"])
```

The keys are "quince", "sreawberry" and "grape" in this dictionary and the values corresponding to these keys are: "yellow", "red" and "green". We have accessed the value of the key "strawberry" with my_dict["strawberry"]. Note that we place the keyi not an index to access the elements (if we compare with lists and tuples). The output of this code segment is as follows:

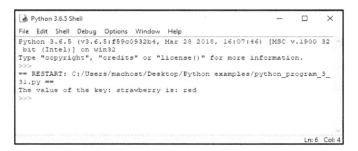

Figure 3.85. Accessing the value of a key in a dictionary

There are various methods for dictionaries. For example, the keys() method returns all the keys and the values() method gives all the values included in a dictionary:

```
my_dict={"quince":"yellow", "strawberry":"red",
"grape":"green"}
print("All the keys of this dict are:",
my_dict.keys())
print("All the values of this dict are:",
my_dict.values())
```

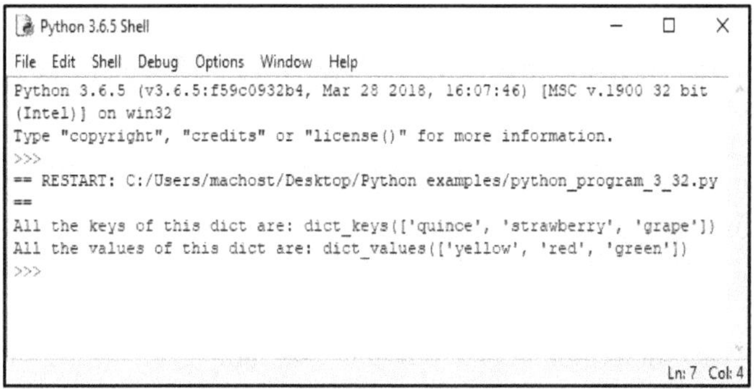

Figure 3.86. Returning the keys and values of a dictionary

The last property of dictionaries I'd like to talk about is that we can add a new key:value pair directly to the dictionary without the need of a special method:

```
my_dict={"quince":"yellow", "strawberry":"red",
"grape":"green"}
my_dict["apricot"]="orange"
print(my_dict)
```

We have inserted the key:value pair of "apricot":"orange" to the dictionary in the second line in this program. Let's see the output:

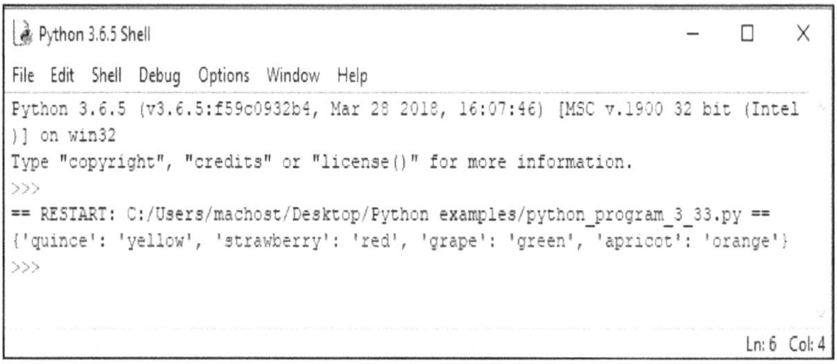

Figure 3.87. The dictionary after a new pair is added

Well, I think this much of Python basics is enough for continuing to the next chapters where we will learn the basics of the programming constructs such as conditional statements and loops. I hope you're enjoying the book and please feel free to contact me anytime if you have questions. I'll be happy to answer all of your quesions in a short time so that you can comfortably continue learning Python in the following chapters.

I'd recommend you to try to do the following exercises so that strenghten your knowledge on Python basics.

3.13. Exercises

1. Take two float numbers from the user and print the sum of these numbers on the screeen.

2. Get a string from the user and print the individual characters of this string seperated by tabs.

3. Ask for 5 numbers from the user, create a list using these numbers and then calculate the average of these numbers to print on the screen. Please use sum() and len() functions on the list.

4. Take a string from the user and print it in uppercase on the screen. (Hint: please find a method for this on the Internet.)

5. Take two numbers from the user, store them in two different variables such as a and b and print them on the screen. Then, swap the values of a and b and then print them again on the screen. (Hint: use a temporary third variable or explore the Internet to find a Pythonic way to swap variables).

Chapter 4. Conditional Statements

We will learn branching our programs accorsing to conditions in this chapter.

4.1. What are conditional statements?

Conditional statements enable the programmers (us!) to branch our program according to the result of a condition as follows:

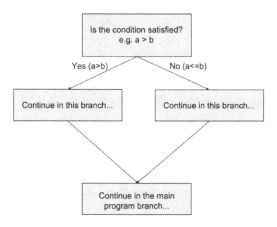

Figure 4.1. General structure of a conditional statement

In this algorithm, if the condition a>b is True such as a=4 and b=2, then the program will continue by the commands written in the left branch. If the condition is not False such as a=2 and b=3, then the commands at the right hand side will be executed.

4.2. Properties of booleans

We have learned that Boolean variables can take the values of either True or False, there is no third option. We use the Booleans in plain or chained form in the conditional statements. Therefore, let's see what we can do with Booleans in Python.

Booleans in fact created when we do a comparison. As you know, comparisons have Boolean results in real life too. For example if we compare two average temperatures like "Is the average temperature of the Canaries higher than that of Stockholm?", the answer is True. Or, "Is the shape of the Earth a cuboid?", the answer is False. As in these examples, we can compare two variables in Python to get a True or False result. And our program will branch accordingly.

There are 6 basic comparison operators in Python whose results are Booleans:

Operator	Operation	Example
>	Returns True if the left hand side variable is greater than the right hand side variable, False otherwise.	3>2 ⇒True 4>10 ⇒False
<	Returns True if the left hand side variable is smaller than the right hand side variable, False otherwise.	-1<0 ⇒True 3.14<1 ⇒False
== (two equal signs)	Returns True if the left hand side variable is equal to the right hand side variable, False otherwise.	0==0.001 ⇒False "Air"=="Air" ⇒True
!=	Returns True if the left hand side variable is not equal to the right hand side variable, False otherwise.	1 != 2 ⇒True a="Python" b="Python" a!=b ⇒False
>=	Returns True if the left hand side variable is greater than or equal to the right hand side variable, False otherwise.	1>=1 ⇒True 2>=3 ⇒False
<=	Returns True if the left hand side variable is smaller than or equal to the right hand side variable, False otherwise.	2<=3 ⇒True 1<=0 ⇒False

Let's do some operations with these operators and print the results on the screen:

```
# The values are defined here
a=4
b=5
c=-7

# Let's do some comparisons
print("a==b is", a==b)
print("b>=c is", b>=c)
print("a<c is: ", a<c)
print("c<=a is:", c<=a)
print("a==b is:", a==b)
```

The results of the comparisons are either True or False:

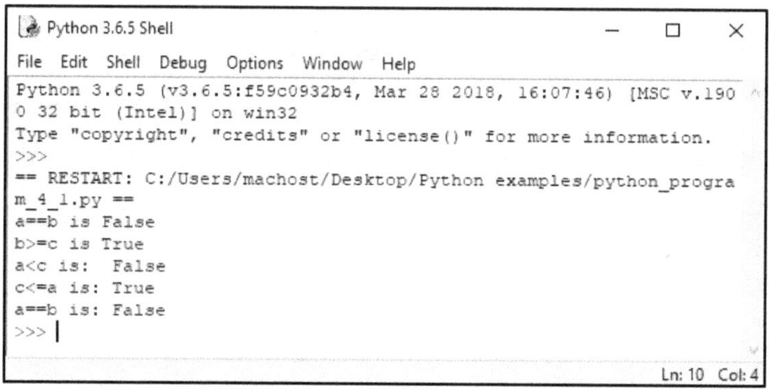

Figure 4.2. Results of comparisons

We sometimes need to check more than one relation among different variables. We can chain the comparisons with logical connections. One of these operators if the *not* operator. It just toggles the Boolean variable it is placed before:

```
a=True
print("The not of a is: ", not a)
```

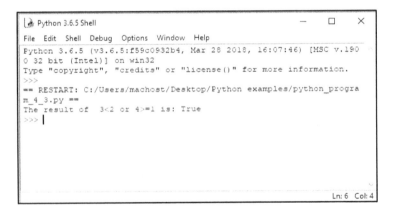

Figure 4.3. The result of a *not* operator

Note that the not operator operates only on one operand, i.e. one variable. Another logical operator is the *or* operator. It operates on two operands and gives True if *at least* one of its operands is True. For example:

```
print("The result of  3<2 or 4>=1 is:", 3<2 or
4>=1)
```

Let's see what Python gives to us:

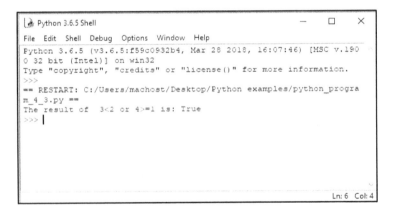

Figure 4.4. Result of an *or* operation

3<2 is False and 4>=1 is True. In this case 3<2 or 4>=1 is *False or True*, which finally evaluates as True according to the *or* operator. The final logic operator we will frequently use is the *and* operator. It gives

True if both of its operands are True and False otherwise. Let's try the same operands using the *and* operator:

```
print("The result of  3<2 and 4>=1 is:", 3<2 and
4>=1)
```

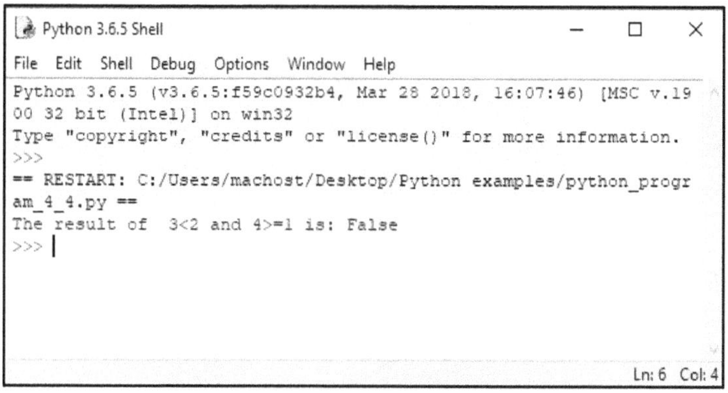

Figure 4.5. The result of an and operation

Since *3<2 and 4>=1* is *False and True*, it evaluates to False since bot of the operands are not True.

We are now ready to see how we will use the results of the logical operations for checking conditions and branching accordingly.

4.3. *If* blocks

The first conditional structure we will use is the *if block*. We use *if blocks* if we will check a condition and run code segments if that condition is satisfied (True). The structure of an if block is as follows:

if (condition):

> *The code lines*

> *in his indented block*

> *are executed if and only if*

> *the condition above is True*

other commands... (will be executed regardless of the condition)

Important: The blocks are written as indented in Python. The indentation is is four spaces (a tab) from the left. When you place a semicolon after the condition and press the Enter key for the new line, the IDLE editor will automatically adjust the indentation.

There are two possibilities:

1. If the (condition) is True, the code lines in the indented if block are executed and then other commands, which are below the if block, are exected.
2. If the condition is False, the commands in the indented block are not executed. And then, other commands which are below the if block, are exected.

Note that the commands that follow the if block shown as other commands are executed independent of the if block.

Let's see the operation fo an if block in an example program:

```
a=4
b=5
if (a<b):
    print("The condition a<b is met and the
    indented block is executed here.")

    print("Here's a command below the first if
    block.")
if (a==b):
    print("The condition a==b is satisfied and the
    corresponding if block is now executed.")

print("The line after the second if block. And also
the end of the program.")
```

Since a=4 nd b=5, the condition of the first if block is True. Then its block will be executed. After the first if block is over, the line print("Here's a command below the first if block.") will be executed independent of any condition since it is not indented and a part of the main program flow. And then the second if block will be checked. Since a is not equal to b, its condition is False and the command inside its block print("The condition a==b is satisfied and the corresponding if block is now executed.") will not be executed. And finally, the line print("The line after the second if block. And also the end of the program.") will be executed indepenedent of any if blocks and the program will exit. Let's see the output of our program:

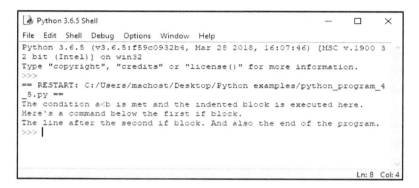

Figure 4.6. The output of our first program using if statements

Let's change the value of the variable a as 5 which will make a<b False and a==b to be True. Now, the first if block will not be executed and the second if block will be executed:

```
a=5
b=5

if (a<b):
    print("The    condition    a<b    is    met    and    the
indented block is executed here.")

print("Here's a command below the first if block.")

if (a==b):
    print("The condition a==b is satisfied and the
corresponding if block is now executed.")

print("The line after the second if block. And also
the end of the program.")
```

The result of our modified program is as follows:

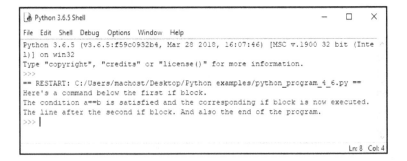

Figure 4.7. The result of our modified program with if blocks

4.4. *If-else* blocks

We have learned the utilization of if blocks. The statements in if blocks are executed if the condition is True. We can add an else block to an if block, which will be executed if the condition is False:

if (condition):

> *The code lines*

> *in his indented block*

> *are executed if and only if*

> *the condition above is True*

else:

> *The code lines*

> *in his indented block*

> *are executed if and only if*

> *the condition above is False*

other commands... (will be executed regardless of the condition)

Please note the difference of the else block and *other commands* below the if structure. The executions of the blocks inside the if and else blocks are dependent on the condition while the execution of *other commands* followinf the if-else structure are independent of the condition, i.e. certainly executed.

Let's use the if-else structure by comparing a predetermined value to an input we get from the user:

```
result="Tails"

user_input=input("Please guess the result of a coin
toss (Tails or Heads): ")

if result==user_input:
    print("Yes, you guessed correctly. It is a",
result)
else:
    print("That's incorrect. It was", result)
```

If the user enters "Tails" string, the condition will be met and the if block will be executed. Else, the block in the else will be executed:

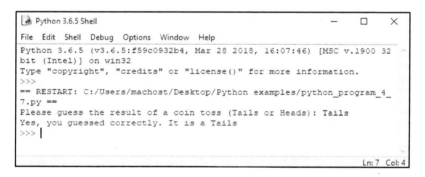

Figure 4.8. The condition is met and the if block is executed

If the user enters something else, the else block will be executed as shown in Figure 4.9.

```
Python 3.6.5 Shell                                    —    □    ×
File  Edit  Shell  Debug  Options  Window  Help
Python 3.6.5 (v3.6.5:f59c0932b4, Mar 28 2018, 16:07:46) [MSC v.1900 32
bit (Intel)] on win32
Type "copyright", "credits" or "license()" for more information.
>>>
== RESTART: C:/Users/machost/Desktop/Python examples/python_program_4_
7.py ==
Please guess the result of a coin toss (Tails or Heads): Heads
That's incorrect. It was Tails
>>> |
                                                        Ln: 7  Col: 4
```

Figure 4.9. The user entered an incorrect guess and the else block is executed

4.5. *If-elif-else* blocks

We may also have to check more than one conditions in a chained manner. We need to use if-elif-else structure in these cases. elif keyword is a short form of else if in Python as follows:

if (condition 1):

>   *The code lines*
>   *in his indented block*
>   *are executed if and only if*
>   *condition 1 is True*

elif (condition 2):

>   *The code lines*
>   *in his indented block*
>   *are executed if and only if condition 1 is False and*
>   *condition 2 is True*

elif (condition 3):

>   *The code lines*

in his indented block

are executed if and only if conditions 1&2 are False and

condition 3 is True

else:

The code lines

in his indented block

are executed if and only if

none of the conditions above are True

We can chain any number of conditions with the if-elif-else chain. For example, let's get the temperature input from the user and compare the temperature value against the table shown below:

Temperature range (°C)	Comment
Less than 0	Very cold
Between 0 and 18	Cold
Between 18 and 25	Normal
Between 25 and 35	Hot
Above 35	Very hot

Our program will be as follows:

```
temp=input("Please enter the temperature value in C:")

temp=float(temp) # Since the user input is always a string type, we need to
                  # convert to a numbertype
for numerical comparisons

if temp < 0:
    print("It's very cold.")
elif temp < 18:
    print("It's cold.")
```

```
elif temp < 25:
    print("It's nice.")
elif temp < 35:
    print("It's hot.")
else:
    print("It's very hot.")
```

For example, if we enter 5 in this program, the first condition will not be satisfied and the conditional chain will check the second condition. It will be met as 5<18 therefore the second block in the chain (print("It's cold.")) will be executed and the if-elif-else block will finish, i.e. the next conditions will not be checked:

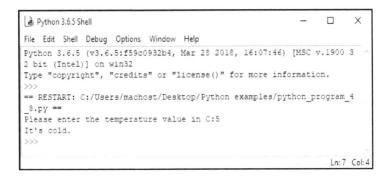

Figure 4.10. The second block is executed as the second condition is satisfied

Please note the requirement to use the elif structure instead of many if structures in these situations. If we used ifs instead of elifs, all the conditions would be checked from top to down and the program would give wrong results:

```
#Wrong algorithm-demonstrates the impoeratnce of
the elif structure
temp=input("Please enter the temperature value in
C:")

temp=float(temp)

if temp < 0:
```

```
      print("It's very cold.")
if temp < 18:
      print("It's cold.")
if temp < 25:
      print("It's nice.")
if temp < 35:
      print("It's hot.")
else:
      print("It's very hot.")
```

If we enter 5 again to this wrong program, it will give the following incorrect result:

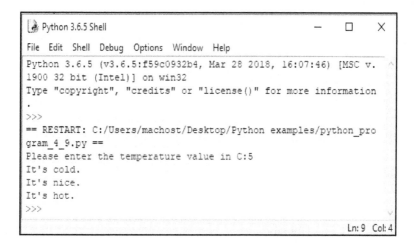

Figure 4.11. The output of the incorrect program

As temp=5 satisfies all three conditions, i.e. temp < 18, temp < 25 and temp < 35, all these blocks are executed making our program incorrect. Therefore we generally need to use the elif blocks when we need to check various conditions on a single variable.

Please also pay attention at the else block in the if-elif-else structure. The else block is executed if none of the above conditions are true. For example, if we enter temperature as 36 in our correct program (program with if-elif-else structure), this value does not satisfy any of the conditions hence the else block will be executed:

```
Python 3.6.5 Shell                                    —    □    ×
File  Edit  Shell  Debug  Options  Window  Help
Python 3.6.5 (v3.6.5:f59c0932b4, Mar 28 2018, 16:07:46) [MSC v.1900 32
bit (Intel)] on win32
Type "copyright", "credits" or "license()" for more information.
>>>
== RESTART: C:\Users\machost\Desktop\Python examples\python_program_4_8
.py ==
Please enter the temperature value in C:36
It's very hot.
>>>
                                                            Ln: 7  Col: 4
```

Figure 4.12. The else block is executed if none of the conditions in if and elifs are True

These are the conditional statements that we will use in our Python programs. Please try to write the programs given in the Exercises section below so that you can strenghten your knowledge on conditionals. After then, we can continue to learning loops in the next chapter.

4.6. Exercises

1. Write a program and get a number from the user to tell if the number is positive, negative or zero. Please try to use if-elif-else structure.

2. Take three numbers from the user and sort them in ascending order.

3. Write a program which will take the current year and will print if February has 28 or 29 days.

4. Write a progran to take a number from the user and tell that if the number is even or odd (we first need to check if the entered number is integer or float. If the number is float, the program will tell the user that it cannot tell if the number is even or odd.)

5. Write a program that will take the current hour from the user and print if it is morning, afternoon, evening or night. (Alternatively, you can also take the current hour automatically in Python! Although we haven't learned yet, you can search as "get current hour python" on the Internet and see how you can easily do it in Pythonic way.)

Chapter 5. Loops

5.1. What is a loop?

We sometimes need some portion of our programs to repeat when a specific condition is satisfied. This is achieved using loops. As in the conditional statements, the loops also have blocks. In the if-else structure, the if block or the else block was executed depending on the condition. In loops, the loop block is repeatadly executed as long as the condition is satisfied. This means that the condition has to be modified inside the loop block so that the number of repetitions of a loop would be finite, otherwise the loop would becomes an infinite loop which makes our programs stuck.

5.2. The *while* loop

The general structure of a while loop is as follows:

while (condition):

> *commands in the*
>
> *while block will*
>
> *be executed until*
>
> *the condition becomes*
>
> *False*

Let's analyze a simple while loop example as follows:

```
a=0
while a<20:
    print("Current value of a is", a)
    a += 1

print("The loop ended.")
```

The value of a is set as 0 at the beginning. The commands in the while loop (again, an indented block) will be executed as if a is less than 20 (a<20). In the beginning a=0 therefore the command in the loop will execute. First, the print statement will print the current value of a as 0. Then the expression a += 1 will increment a by one making the new value of a to be 1. Then the loop condition will be checked again. Since a is still less than 20, the command in the loop block will be executed again and the new value of a will be 2. This will continue until a=20. When a=20, the loop condition will be broken and then looping will end. The las line which is after the loop will be executed and the program will exit:

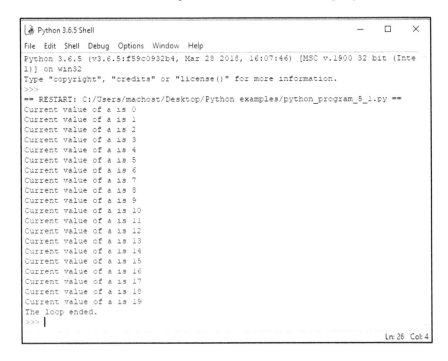

Figure 5.1. Output of our program utilizing a while loop

We increment the loop variable a so that at some point the loop will exit. In the above example we incremented it by one in each loop (a += 1). We can modify the loop variable per our need, not necessarily incrementing by 1. For example, let's increment a by 5 in each loop:

```
a=0
while a<20:
    print("Current value of a is", a)
    a += 5

print("The loop ended.")
```

The output of this program will show that a is incremented by 5 in each loop:

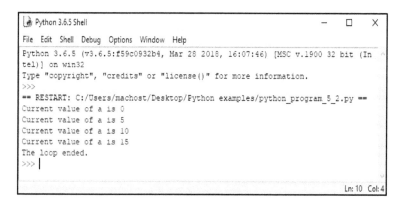

Figure 5.2. The same loop incrementing the value of a by 5

Note that *Current value of a is 20* is not executed as the a=20 breaks the loop condition (a<20) and the loop has exited before executing this command.

If we fail to make the loop condition False at some point, the loop continues forever and forms an infinite loop. For example, if we forget incrementing the value of the loop variable, we form an infinite loop:

```
a=0
while a<20:
    print("Current value of a is", a)

print("The loop ended.")
```

Since the value of will not be updated, the loop will continue printing `Current value of a is 0` forever. I have done the dangerous thing: executed this program in IDLE (infinte loop WARNING: don't try at home, or you can try and just press Ctrl+C together to force quit the IDLE prompt):

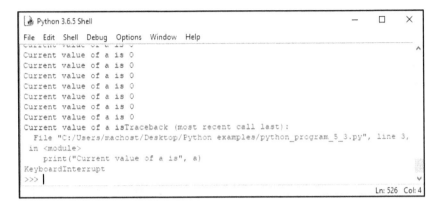

Figure 5.2. The infinite loop tried to print *Current value of a is 0* infinitely until I have beaten it by pressing Ctrl+C

Another possible situation where an infinite loop occurs is setting the loop condition incorrectly. For example:

```
a=1
while a>0:
    print("Current value of a is", a)
    a += 1

print("The loop ended.")
```

Since the value of a will always be greater than 0, the loop condition will always be True and the loop will continue forever (until we press Ctrl+C haha) as shown in Figure 5.4.

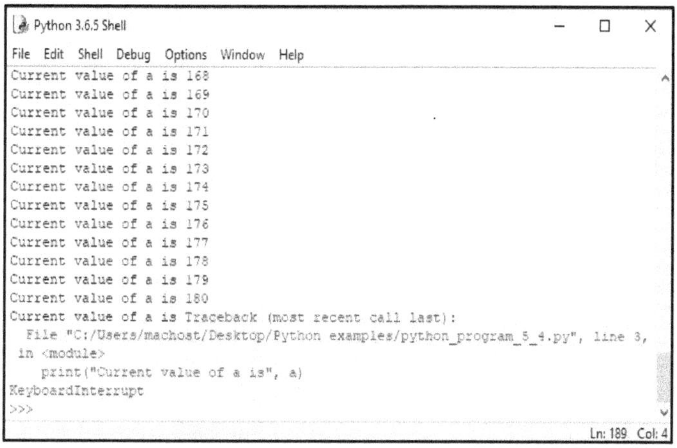

Figure 5.4. Another infinite loop beaten by Ctrl+C

Therefore, we should be extra careful about the loop conditions to avoid infinite loops.

5.3. The *break* and *continue* keywords

The `break` and `continue` keywords are used for controlling the behaviour of loops. When a `break` statement is executed in a loop, the loop exits immediately without checking the state of the loop variable:

```
a=0
while a<11:
    if a==5:
        print("The break statement will be executed
now.")
        break
    print("Current value of a is", a)
    a += 1

print("Loop finished.")
```

The loop would print the values of a as 0,1...,10. However, when a=5, the condition of the if statement becomes True and the commands inside the if statement are executed, including the `break` statement. Therefore, the loop ends immediately when a=5:

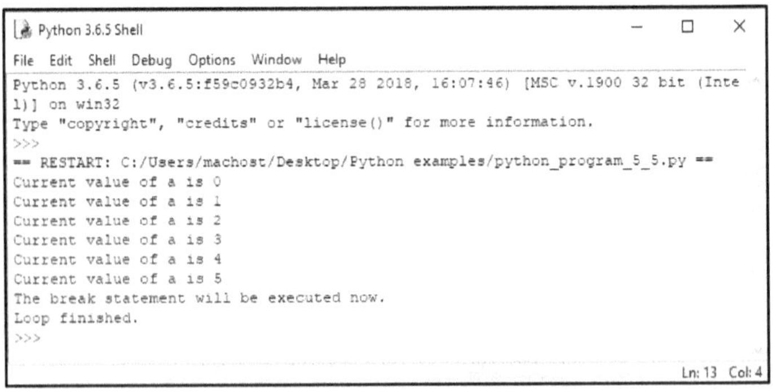

Figure 5.5. The `break` keyword broke the loop

We can also use the `True` keyword as the loop condition to intentionally make an infinite loop and use the break statement to control the loop as follows: :

```
while True:
    user_input=input("Please enter the password:")
    if user_input == "12345":
        print("Correct password.")
        break
    print("Incorrect password!! Please try
again...")
```

Since the loop condition is set as True, the while loop is expected to execute indefinitely. However, if the user enters the correct password, the commands in the if statement will execute breaking the infinite cycle:

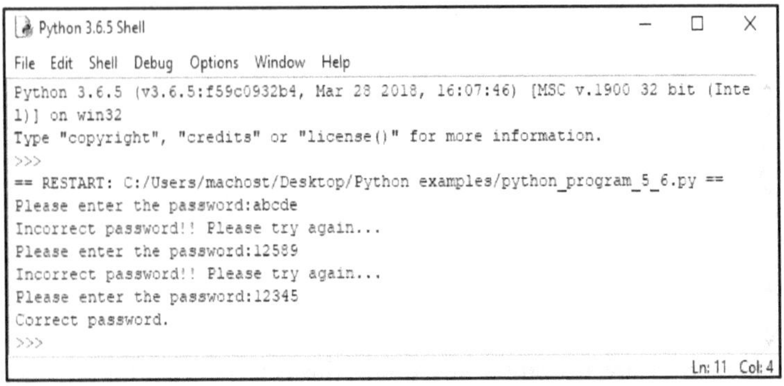

Figure 5.6. The loop continues until the correct password is entered

Another useful command used in conjunction with loops is the `continue` keyword. Its operation is similar to the break statement. However, instead of finishing the loop, the continue command makes the the program to skip the current iteration of the loop and continue with the next iteration:

```
a=0
while a<10:
    if a==4:
        a += 1
        print("The commands under this point will
be skipped.\nThe
                loop will continue with the next
value.")
        continue
    print("Current value of a is", a)
    a += 1

print("The loop ended.")
```

In this example, when a=4, the if block will be executed which contains a continue statement. The execution of the current loop will be skipped and continut with the next iteration:

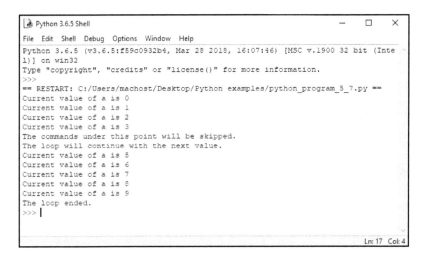

Figure 5.7. *continue* statement skipped the loop at a=4

5.4. The *for* loop

Another type of loop in Python is the for loop. The for loop enables us to sweep over a list, tuple or dictionary structure easily without the need for managing the loop variable. In order to observe the ease provided by the for loop, let's first try to sweep over a list using the while loop:

```python
my_list=[1,2,4,5,8,9,11,15]
i=0 # The loop variable
while i<len(my_list):
    print("The   {}th   element   of   the   list   is:
{}".format(i, my_list[i]))
    i += 1
```

Here, we defined a loop variable i and swept it from 0 to the number which is (length of my_list-1) and printed the value of the ith element in each iteration:

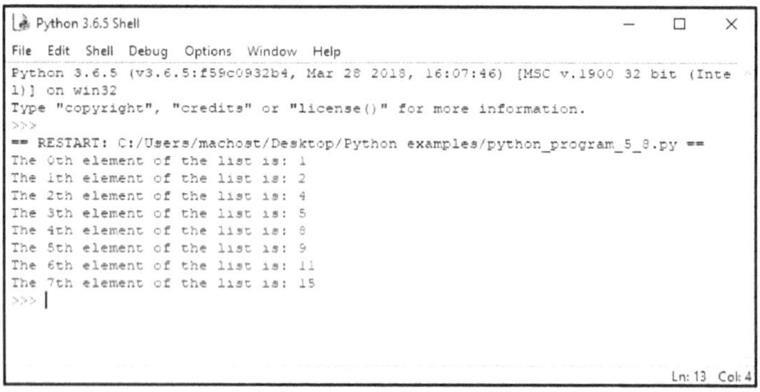

Figure 5.8. Sweeping over the elements of a list using a while loop and managing a loop variable

The same program can be re-written using the for loop as follows:

```python
my_list=[1,2,4,5,8,9,11,15]
for member in my_list:
    print("The current element of the list is:",
    member)
```

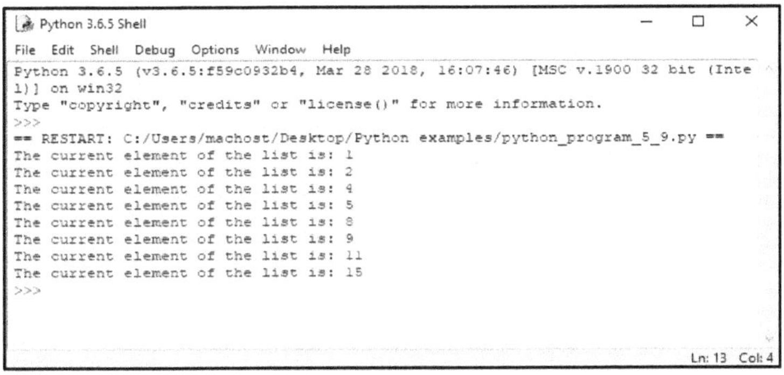

Figure 5.9. Sweeping over the list elements using the for loop

The general structure of a for loop is s follows:

for member in list:

> *Commands in the loop (typically using the current member of the loop)*

We can also sweep over strings using the for loop:

```
my_string="Hello"
for current_char in my_string:
    print(current_char)
```

The for loop iterates the string's each element (character) and prints on the screen:

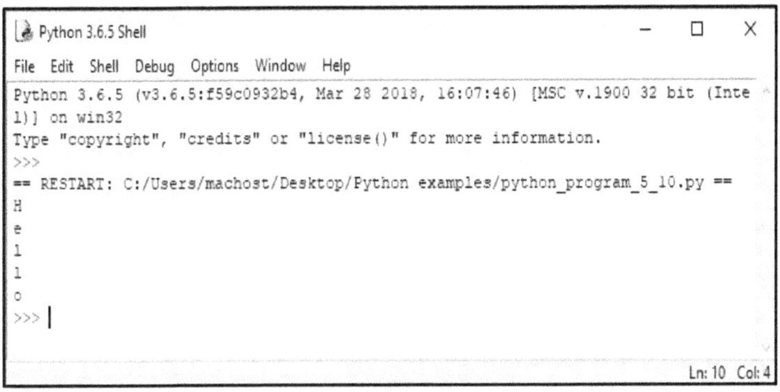

Figure 5.10.Sweeping a string using a for loop

5.5. The *range()* function

The for loop can also be used for iteratiiong over tuples and dictionaries but this is rarely used. On the other hand, we can also form a number sequence using a built-in function called range() and iterate over this sequence using the for loop. The usage of the range() function is as follows:

sequence=range(start, stop, step(optional))

Let's form a sequence using the range function and print it:

```
sequence=range(0,10)
print(*sequence)
```

Note that we used the * operator here to split the values of the sequence for printing on the screen (remember that we used the * operator in strings too). Also note that the last value specified in the range function is not included in the sequence:

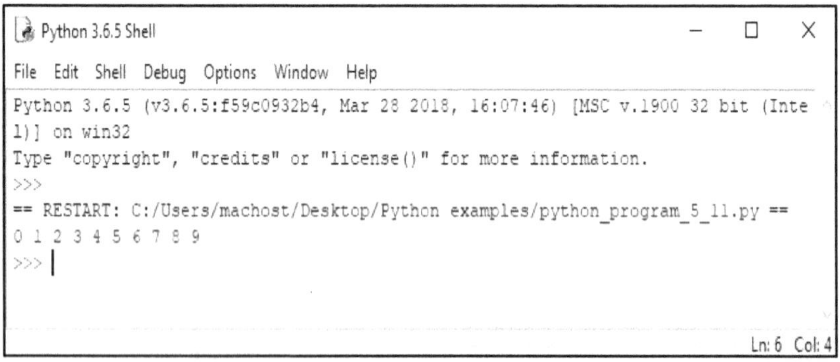

Figure 5.11. The output sequence of the range function

We can iterate over the elements of a range() function as follows:

```
for i in range(0,10,2):
    print(i)
```

In this program, we created a sequence using the range() function which goes from 0 to 9 with step=2, therefore the sequence returned by range(0,10,2) is 0,2,4,6,8. Let's try this in Python:

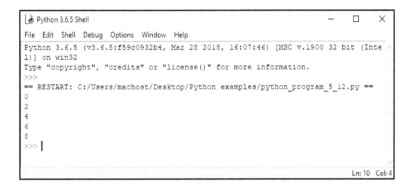

Figure 5.12. Elements of the sequence returned by the range(0,10,2) function is printed using a for loop

That's all about the loops in Python. Please try to write the programs given in the exercises below before continuing to the next chapter where we will see writing our own functions in Python.

5.6. Exercises

1. The factorian of a number n is defined as n!=n.(n-1).(n-2)...2.1. For example, 6!=6.5.4.3.2.1=720. Please write a program that asks for an integer from the user and calculates and prints the factorial of that number.

2. Write a program that calculates and prints the sum of first 100 positive integers.

3. Write a program that will ask for the grades of 20 students and will calculate the average of these grades.

4. Write a program that will calculate the greatest common divisor of two numbers entered by the user.

5. Write a program that will print the integers from n to 0 in the reverse order such as if n=6, the program will print 6,5,4,3,2,1,0. The value of n will be entered by the user.

Chapter 6. Functions

6.1. Introduction to functions

Functions are structures which enable us to group a group of code for later re-use or share with other programmers. Python has around 70 built-in functions which were written by Python developers and shared with us to use in our programs. An example is the built-in input() function we used in numerous programs.

We will learn how to define our own functions in Python in this chapter.

6.2. Defining functions

We use the def keyword to define a custom function as follows:

def function_name(parameters (optional)):

    commands in the

    function block are

    executed from top to down as usual

    return a value (optional)

Here, the function block will be written as indented as we did in other structures (if, for) before. The function may or may not take parameters from the user. If the function will not get any value from the user, inside of the parantheses will be empty. Also, the function may or may not return a value. If the function will not return a value, we will not use the return keyword. Let's define our first custom function which doesn't accept any parameter and doesn't return any value:

```
def welcome():
    print("Welcome to the space-age programming
    language: Python!
```

When we define this function in our program, and run out source file, we will not see anything on the prompt:

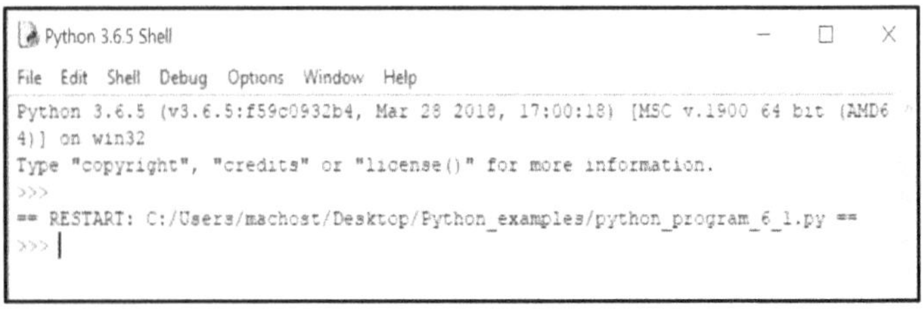

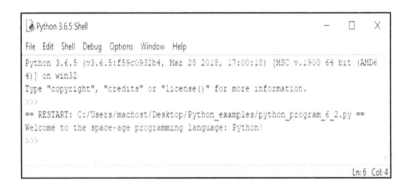

Figure 6.1. We don't get anything when we execute the program in ewhich we defined our first function

The prompt says that our program is executed but didn't print anything. This is because functions are executed only if they are called (invoked). We simply shout the name of the function to call it:

```python
def welcome():
    print("Welcome to the space-age programming
    language: Python!")

# Let's call our welcome() function:
```

Figure 6.2. The output of our program when we call our function

We called our function by the line welcome() and the function block is executed. Since there's only the print("Welcome to the space-age programming language: Python!") command in the function block, the text "Welcome to the space-age programming language: Python!" is written by Python.

We can call our function as many times as we need and at any line in our program (of course after the function is defined):

```
def welcome():
    print("Welcome   to   the   space-age   programming
language: Python!")

# Let's call our welcome() function:

welcome()
welcome()
welcome()
welcome()
welcome()
```

We called our function 5 times in the program and the function block will be executed 5 times accordingly:

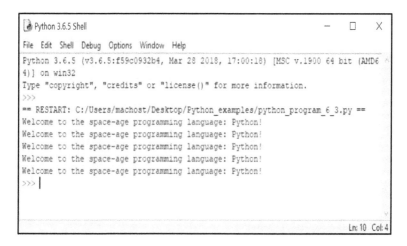

Figure 6.3. We called our welcome() function 5 times consecutively

6.3. Functions with parameters

We usually need our functions to perform operations according to some parameters (values). In this case we design our function to accept inputs as follows:

```
def new_year(year):
    print("Welcome", year, "!!!")

# Let's give 2019 and 2020 to the new_year()
function:

new_year("2019")
new_year("2020")
```

We have defined the new_year() function which accepts the *year* variable as the parameter and prints the corresponding welcome message. Then, we called this function with two different parameters:

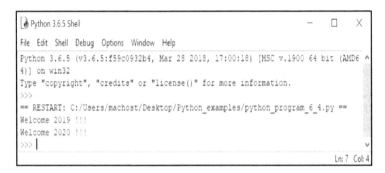

Figure 6.4. Calling a function with different parameters

We can also use multiple parameters in functions using commas between them:

```
def product(x,y,z):
    print("The product of {}, {} and {} is
{}".format(x,y,z,x*y*z))

product(3,5,7)
```

This function accepts three parameters x,y,z and prints the product of these parameters. Note these parameters are considered as numerical values as we have given them as integers to the function at the last line. Here's the output of this program:

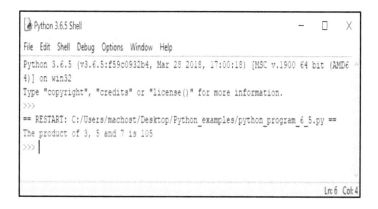

Figure 6.5. Using multiple parameters in a function

Sometimes we may need to attach a default value for parameter(s) of a function. We do this as in the following example:

```python
def power(number, power=2):
    print("{}    to    the    power    of    {}    is
{}".format(number, power, number**power))

power(3)
```

This function calculates and prints the number to the power of power: number^{power}. The default value of power is set as 2 therefore in the power(3) line, the value of power is taken as its default value:2. On the other hand, when we call the function with two parameters as in power(3,3), the default value of power is overwritten by 3 and our function calculates 3^3 in this case as shown in Figure 6.6.

```
Python 3.6.5 Shell                                    —  □  X

File  Edit  Shell  Debug  Options  Window  Help

Python 3.6.5 (v3.6.5:f59c0932b4, Mar 28 2018, 17:00:18) [MSC v.1900 64 bit (AMD6
4)] on win32
Type "copyright", "credits" or "license()" for more information.
>>>
== RESTART: C:/Users/machost/Desktop/Python_examples/python_program_6_6.py ==
3 to the power of 2 is 9
3 to the power of 3 is 27
>>>

                                                              Ln: 7  Col: 4
```

Figure 6.6. Using and overwriting the default value of a parameter of a function

6.4. Functions with indefinite number of parameters

Python is a flexible language. We can also define functions which accepts any number of parameters using a list structure:

```python
def multiply(*input_list):
    product=1
    for i in input_list:
        product *= i
    print("The    product    of    the    elements    of",
input_list, "is", product)

multiply(1,3,5)
```

We send a list of numbers as the parameter to the function here. And then, we iterate over the elements of this list using a for loop and multiply each element with the product variable making the final value of this variable to be the product of the list's elements. Finally, we print the product. We called this function with two lists with different number of elements and got their products as follows in Figure 6.7.

```
Python 3.6.5 Shell                                    —   □   ✕

File  Edit  Shell  Debug  Options  Window  Help
Python 3.6.5 (v3.6.5:f59c0932b4, Mar 28 2018, 17:00:18) [MSC v.1900 64 bit (AMD6
4)] on win32
Type "copyright", "credits" or "license()" for more information.
>>>
== RESTART: C:/Users/machost/Desktop/Python_examples/python_program_6_7.py ==
The product of the elements of (1, 3, 5) is 15
The product of the elements of (1, 3, 5, 10) is 150
>>> |

                                                                    Ln: 7  Col: 4
```

Figure 6.7. Using a function with lists as a parameter

6.5. Functions with return values

Until here, our functions did not return any value, they performed operations and printed the results on the screen. However, we may need to get the calculated values from functions and assign them to some variables in our program. We use the return keyword for this type of operations:

```
def sum(a,b):
    c=a+b # c is some variable inside the function
block
    return c  # the value of c is returned

#Let's call our function and assign the returned
value to a new variable

x=sum(4,5)
print("The returned value is", x)
```

In this function, we created a new variable, c, inside the function block and returned its value. And in the main program, we called our function with parameters of 4 and 5 and assigned the returned value to x, and finally printed the value of x:

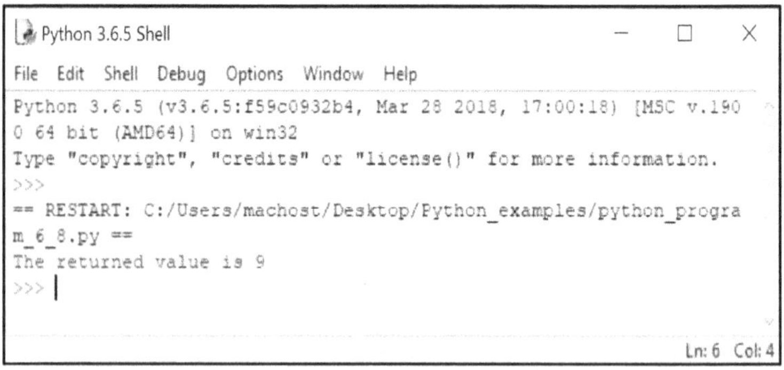

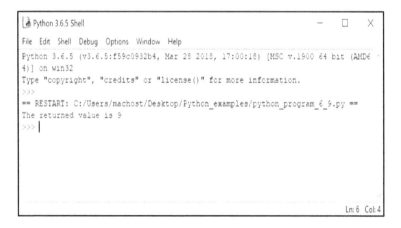

Figure 6.8. The returned value is assigned to x and the printed on the screen

We can also directly print the returned value without the need of assigning it to a new variable:

```
def sum(a,b):
    c=a+b # c is some variable inside the function
block
    return c  # the value of c is returned

#Let's call our function and assign directly print
the returned value
```

The result is the same as before:

Figure 6.9. Directly printing the returned value of a function

We can also return multiple values as follows:

```
def operations(a,b):
    return a+b, a*b

add, product= operations(2,3)
print("The sum and the product of {} and {} is {}
and {}.".format(2,3,add,product))
```

We assigned the returned sequence to the add, product structure and then printed the result at the last line:

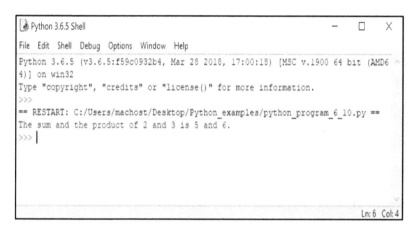

Figure 6.10. Returning multiple values from a function

6.6. Local and global variables of functions

We have created variables inside function blocks. These variables are local to the function block and cannot be accessed from our main program flow. They are created during the execution of a function and destroyed when the operation of the function completes. If we try to access a local variable from our main program, we get an error:

```
def sum(a,b):
    c=a+b
    return c

print("The sum of 3 and 4 is", sum(3,4))
print(c)
```

The program will execute fine until the last line where we try to access variable c, which was already destroyed after the function exit:

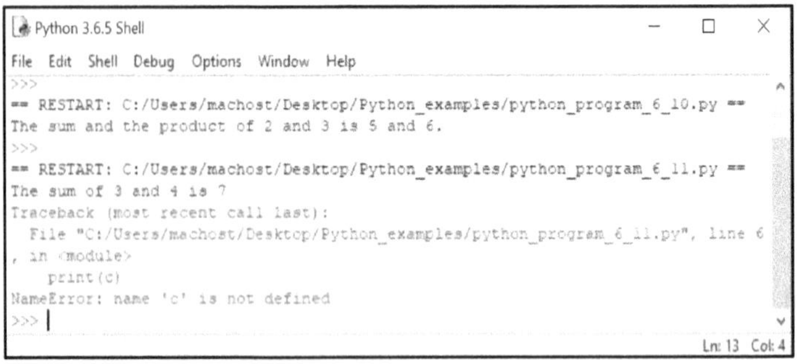

Figure 6.11. Trying to access a local variable gives an error

In rare cases, we may strive to access the variables inside the function block. In these cases, we use the global keyword so that the variables becomes global variables instead of local variables and can be accessed from anywhere in our main code:

```
def sum(a,b):
    global c
    c=a+b
    return c

print("The sum of 3 and 4 is", sum(3,4))
```

We can now access and print the value of c:

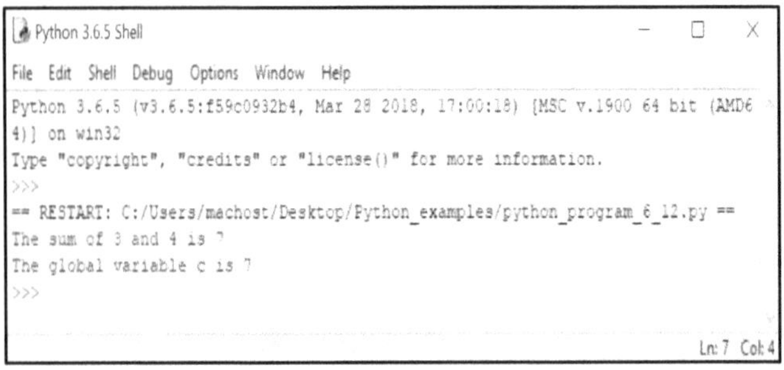

Figure 6.12. Accessing the global variable from the main program

Note that the variables inside conditional statements and loops are global variables while the variables inside function blocks are local variables bu default.

6.7. Defining functions in a single line of code (*lambda* expressions)

We can define functions in a single line using the *lambda* keyword. The template of this type of definition is as follows:

function_name = lambda parameters of the function: expression to be evaluated and returned

Let's define a function as usual:

```
def sum(x,y):
    return x+y

print("The sum of 2 and 3 is:", sum(2,3))
```

Let's rewrite this function using the lambda keyword:

```
sum = lambda x,y: x+y

print("The sum of 2 and 3 is:", sum(2,3))
```

The output of both programs are the same as expected:

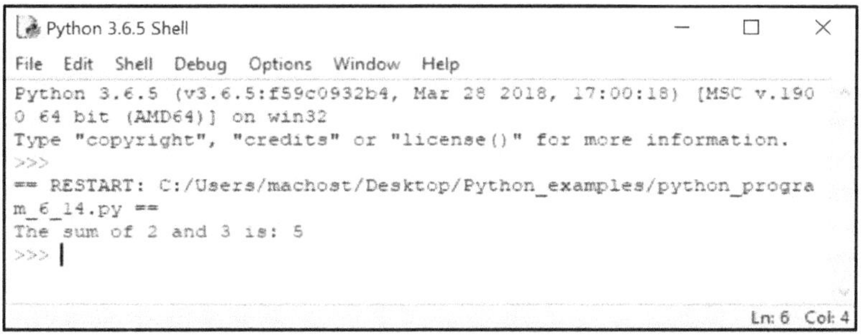

Figure 6.13. Output of the program using our single-line function definition

The single-line function definitions are especially versatile when the function block is a single line command. We can always use the classical function definition (using the def keyword) in all cases anyway.

We have learned grouping our frequently used commands in functions for organizing our programs and sharing our algorithms in this chapter. In the next chapter, we will see how we can place our code segments and functions in seperate files: modules. But please try to write the functions given in the Exercises below before continuing to the next chapter.

6.8. Exercises

1. Write a function which takes three integers as parameters and returns the average of these numbers. Please use this function in your program.

2. Write a function that accepts a string and retuns the number of spaces in this string. Please use this function in a program.

3. Write a function that takes a list of integers, floats and strings and returns the integers in the list. Please use this function in a program.

4. Write a function that accepts the coefficients of the second order algebraic equation a, b and c for $ax^2+bx+c=0$ and returns the roots of this equation. Please use this function in a program.

5. Write a function that takes the temperature in Celcius and returns the temperature as Fahrenheit. Please use this function in a program. (You can just search Celcius to Fahrenheit on the Internet to find the formula.)

Chapter 7. Modules

7.1. Importing modules – method 1

A module is a single Python source file which contains global variables, functions or classes (we'll learn classes in the next chapter). We can include a module in another Python program so that we can access all elements of the module easily. Python has numerous built-in modules that exist in the (your Python installation directory)\Lib by default. We can import these modules in our programs to use the variables and functions included in these modules. We can simply use the *import* statement to import a module in our program:

import module_name

Let's import the math module, which is a built-in module and access the pi constant existing in this module. Then we'll also access the sin() function:

```
import math

print("Approximate pi is", math.pi)
print("The sine of pi/4 is", math.sin(math.pi/4))
```

In the first line, we imported the math module in our program. In the next line, we printed the approximate value of pi as stored in this module. We accessed the value of this global variable using the dot notation *math.pi*. In the last line, we used the sinus function of the math module: *math.sin()*. We gave the number pi/4 as an argument to the sinus function by using the built-in value of pi: *math.pi/4*. Let's see the output of this program:

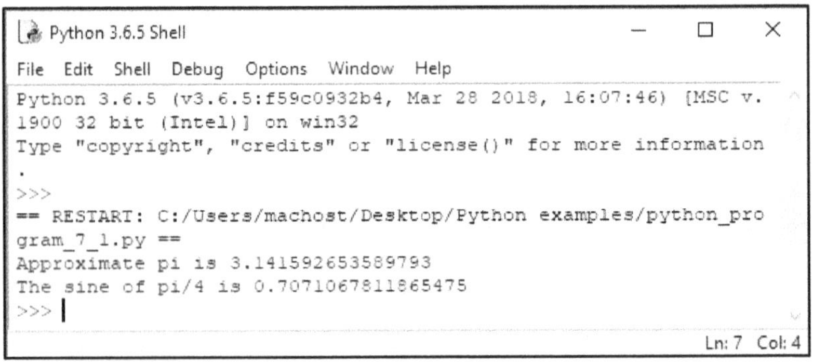

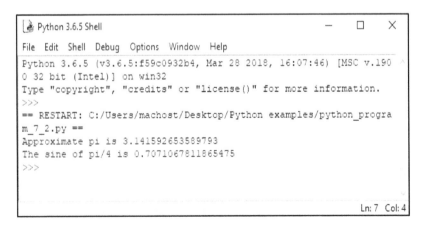

Figure 7.1. Using built-in values and functions of the math module

We could also assign the value of pi to a variable we create in our own program and then use it in the sin() function:

```
import math
own_pi=math.pi
print("Approximate pi is", own_pi)
print("The sine of pi/4 is", math.sin(own_pi))
```

We have defined the variable own_pi in our program and got its value from the math module. We then used this variable in the following code lines. The result will be same as before:

Figure 7.2. The output of our program while using our own variable which got its value from the module

7.2. Importing modules – method 2

We used the dot notation to access the variables and functions of the module when we used the *import module_name* structure for importing the module. We can also provide a direct access to the module's variables and functions by importing everything of the module at once by the following import expression:

from module_name import *

All the functins, variables and classes of the module is imported to our program and we can access them directly without the need for the dot notation in this case:

```
from math import *

print("Approximate pi is", pi)
print("The sine of pi/4 is", sin(pi/4))
```

And viola! We get the same result:

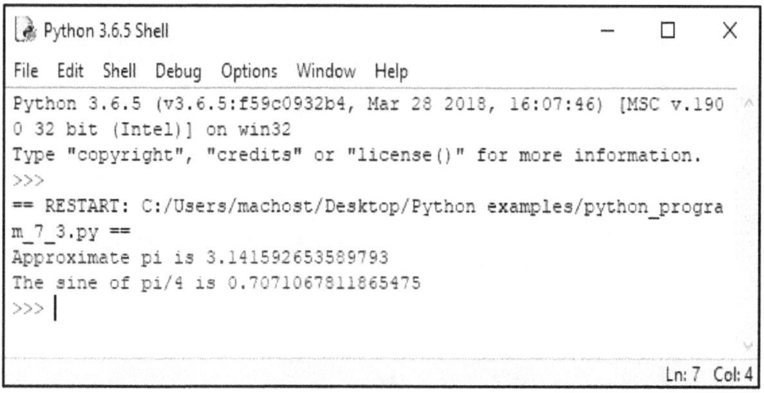

Figure 7.3. Accessing the variables and functions directly

We can always import everything in modules using this method. However, if we will import several modules and they may have variables and functions with the same name, we won't be able to use theses entities properly. Therefore it is always a good practice to import the modules with the first structure, i.e. *import module_name*.

Another method for importing modules is by using the following template:

from module_name import variable_name_1, variable_name_n,..., function_name1, ...function_name_n

In this case, we import some of the variables and functions of the module. Again, we can access the imported variables and functions without the dot notation:

```
from math import e, cos

print("Euler's number is", e)
print("The cos of e is", cos(e))
print("The sin of e is", sin(e))
```

We imported the Euler's number `e` and the cosine function `cos` from the math module in the first line. Then we printed the value of the Euler's number and cos(e) in the next two code lines. We don't expect any problems here. However, in the last line, we tried to use the sin() function which wasn't imported to our program therefore the sin() function is an unidentified function for our program. Python will issue the corresponding error saying that the name 'sin' is not defined:

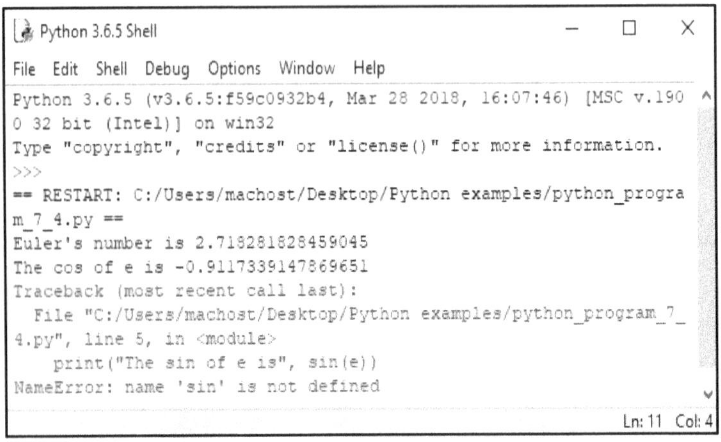

Figure 7.4. Python gives an error if we try to use a function that wasn't imported

How can we see which variables, functions and classes are available to us in a specific module and their descriptions? We can use the help() function of Python after importing the corresponding module. For example, let's see the contents of a built-in module called email which is useful for parsing and manipulating email messages. We will firstly import the email module and type help(email) in the IDLE prompt:

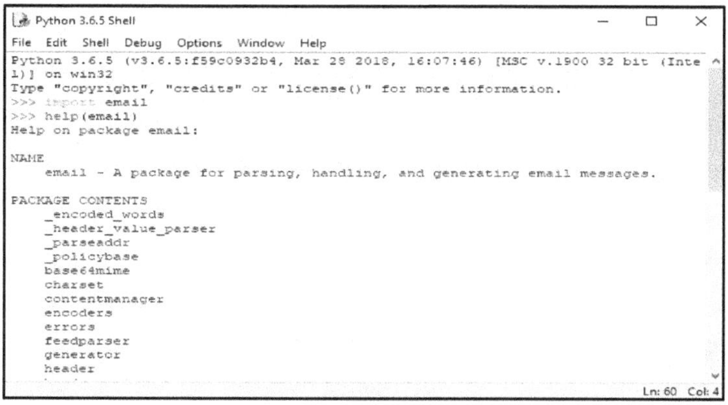

Figure 7.5. Importing the email module and viewing its contents (1)

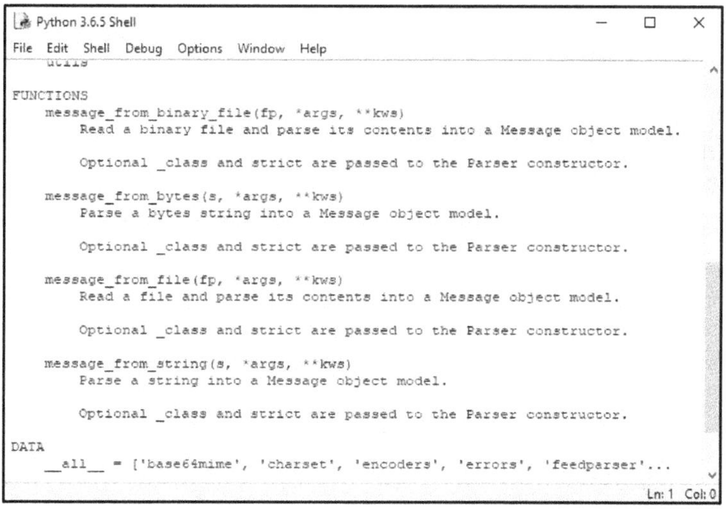

Figure 7.6. Importing the email module and viewing its contents (2)

7.3. Writing our own modules

We can also write our own modules and import them in other programs. For example, let's create a new file in the IDLE Editor and place the following variables and functions inside it:

```
room_temp = 25

def comp(T1):
    if T1 > room_temp:
        print("Current    temperature    {}    is    greater
than the room temperature.".format(T1))
    elif T1 < T2:
        print("Current temperature {} is lower than
the room temperature.".format(T1))
    else:
        print("Current temperature {} is at the
ideal room temperature.".format(T1)
```

We can save this file as my_module.py. Now, let's create another file in the IDLE Editor and import the our my_module.py in it:

```
import my_module

temp=30
print("The    ideal    temperature    is    set    as",
my_module.room_temp)
my_module.comp(temp)
```

We need to save this file in the same directory as my_module.py. In this file we have imported our own module and accessed its room_temp variable using the dot structure as *my_module.room_temp*. Then, in the next line we called the function of my_module again with the dot structure my_module.comp(temp). Note that we sent the temp variable of our main program to the function inside the module we called. Lt's run this program to see its output:

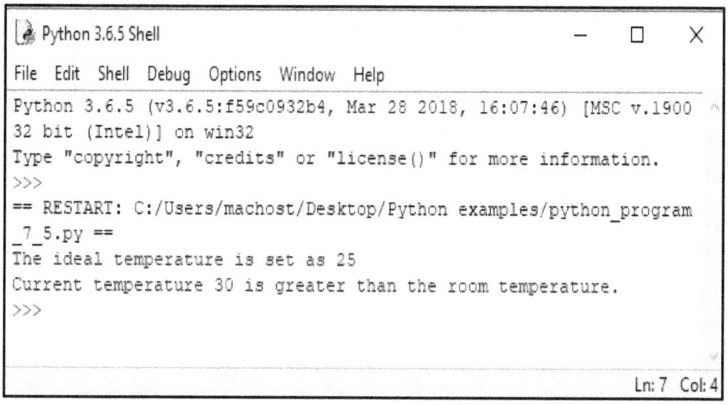

Figure 7.7. Calling a variable and a function from our own module

As we have stated above, we need to place the module file and the program file in the same directory so that the program can find the module. In addition, we can place our own modules inside the *(Python installation folder)/Lib* directory on our computer and the module will be available to all programs we write.

I think this much of information on modules is good for continuing to the next chapter where we will learn managing errors in our Python programs. Please try to solve the following exercises before you proceed to the next chapter.

7.4. Exercises

1. Write a program in which you display the sinus values of the degrees from 0 to 360 in tabular form (Hint: you can create the degree values using the range function such as range(0, 360)).

2. Write a program which will simulate coin tossing 10000 times and report the number of heads and tails (Hint: You can use the built-in random module). See if you can get 5000 Heads and 5000 Tails at different runs of the program.

3. Implement the above program using the *secrets* module instead of the random module and test the difference of the outcomes.

4. Write a function which accepts a string as a parameter and tells the user if it is a keyword in Python (You can use the keyword module).

5. Write a module in which you implement fourth_root() function which accepts a number and returns the 4th order root of that number, i.e. $\sqrt[4]{x}$, then use this module and its function in your program (Hint: You can use the math.sqrt function).

Chapter 8. Error Handling

8.1. Introduction

We have seen that some incorrect commands cause errors in Python and Python issues errors depending on the types of these errors. Some of these errors may be handled so that the program can continue skipping the corresponding errornous code line. These types of conditions which are caught by the application is also called as an *exception*. Some of the errors we sometimes face are "division by zero" which occurs when we try to divide a number by zero; "not defined error" which happens when we try to access a variable before creating it; or "syntax error" when we write the source code incorrectly. There are numerous of error types in Python and we can manage them by error handling mechanisms so that our program can continue skipping the incorrect code lines.

8.2. The basic exception handling structure: *try-except*

The basic exception handling structure is as follows:

try:

   Main code block

   which may contain incorrect commands

except:

   Code block

   that runs if an error occurs

Let's see error handling in a simple example:

```
a=0
b=1
try:
    print("b/a is", b/a)
except:
    print("An error occured.")
```

Since, b=0, Python will not be able to perform b/a and an error will occur in the main code block (try block). Therefore the exception block (except block) will be executed by Python:

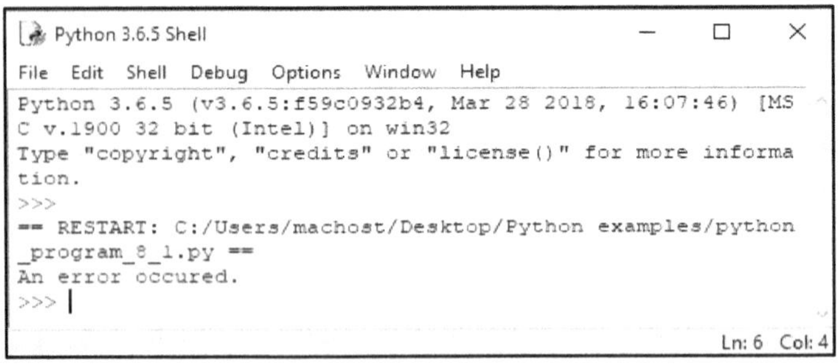

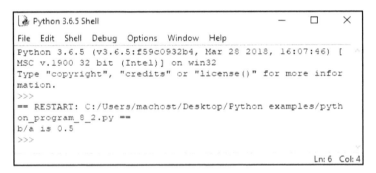

Figure 8.1. Exception block is executed

If we update the value of **a** to a nonzero value such as a=2, then the expression b/a will not be errornous and the main code block (try block) will be executed and the exception block will be ignored:

Figure 8.2. Removing the error causes the try block to execute and the except block is ignored

8.3. Printing information about the exception

In the above example, Python notified us of an error but didn't give any information about the details of the error. We can use the structure:

except Exception as e

to get information about the error:

```
a=0
b=1
try:
    print("b/a is", b/a)
except Exception as e:
    print("The error '{}' is occured.".format(e))
```

If an exception occurs, the information about this exception will be stored in e and will be printed in the except block. Here, the exception is again the division by zero error because a=0, b=1 and we try to execute b/a in the try block. The output of this program is:

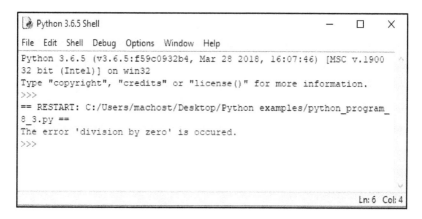

Figure 8.3. The information about the error is printed

Let's change the error in out try block. We can try to access an undefined variable c as an example:

```
a=0
b=1
try:
    print("b/c is", b/c)
except Exception as e:
    print("The error '{}' is occured.".format(e))
```

The error will be different in this case:

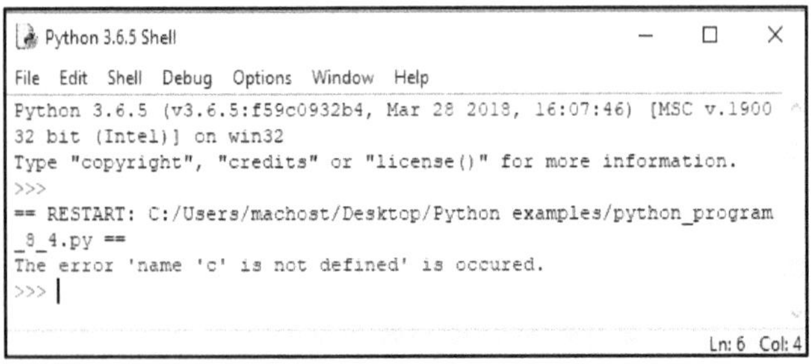

Figure 8.4. Another exception occured in this case

8.4. Utilizing different except blocks for different exceptions

We may need to do separate exception blocks depending on the type of error. We can use multiple except blocks as follows for this type of operation:

try:

   Main code block

   which may contain

   incorrect commands

except error_type_1:

   Code block

   that runs if error_type_1 occurs

except error_type_2:

   Code block

   that runs if error_type_2 occurs

except error_type_3:

   Code block

   that runs if error_type_3 occurs

Let's check two types of errors and *throw an exception* accordingly:

```
a=0
b=1
try:
    print("b/c is", b/c)
except NameError:
    print("Name error occured. There's an undefined
variable.")
```

In the current case we try to do b/c and c is not defined. Therefore, the except block with the NamError will be executed:

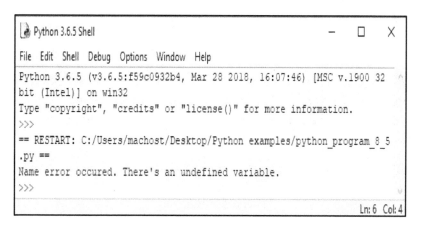

Figure 8.5. Trying to access an undefined variable raises the NameError exception

Let's modify our try block and try to perform b/a where a=0:

```
a=0
b=1
try:
    print("b/c is", b/a)
except NameError:
    print("Name error occured. There's an undefined
variable.")
except ZeroDivisionError:
    print("Divison by zero detected.")
```

This time the exception of zero division occurs and the corresponding exception block is executed:

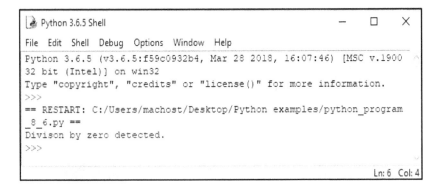

Figure 8.6. Division by zero raises an ZeroDivisionError exception

8.5. The *finally* block

We may need to execute some code lines independent of the exceptions. In other words, we may have some code lines which should be executed independent of the existence of exceptions. We use the *finally* blocks for these code lines:

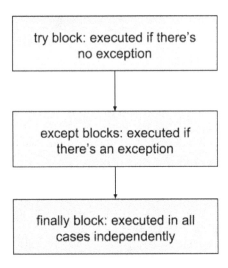

Figure 8.7. The structure of a try-except-finally block

The finally blocks are generally used in functions where we don't want the return statement would terminate the function before mandatory things like closing files or databases:

```python
def func1():
    print("Open a file. Has to be closed before the
program exits.")
    try:
        print("1/0 is", 1/0)
        print("Write to the file.")
        print("File not closed yet.")
        return
    except:
        print("Exception occured.")
        print("Write to the file.")
        print("File not closed yet.")
        return

    print("Closing the file.")
    print("File closed.")
func1()
```

In this example, we have written the virtual file closing line in the main function block. However sinde the function will return in the exception block, the file will remain open when we execute this program:

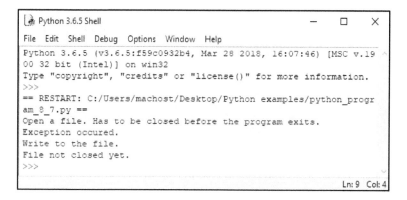

Figure 8.8. Ignoring the finally block causes problems especially in file and database operations

If we place the file closing line inside a *finally* block, we solve this problem:

```python
def func1():
    print("Open a file. Has to be closed before the program exits.")
    try:
        print("1/0 is", 1/0)
        print("Write to the file.")
        print("File not closed yet.")
        return
    except:
        print("Exception occured.")
        print("Write to the file.")
        print("File not closed yet.")
        return
    finally:
        print("Closing the file.")
        print("File closed.")
func1()
```

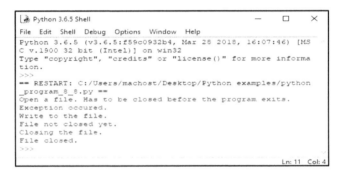

Figure 8.9. Guaranteeing the file cloing operation with a *finally* block

8.6. Raising custom exceptions

We can also raise our own exceptions using the raise keyword. Please consider the following example:

```python
def func2(input1, input2):
    if input1 % input2 !=0:
        raise    ValueError("{}    is    not    integer
divisible by {}.".format(input1, input2))
```

```
        else:
            return int(input1/input2)
try:
    print(func2(6,3))
except Exception as e:
    print(e)
```

The exception will be raised with the string "{} is not integer divisible by {}.".format(input1, input2) if input1 is not integer divisible by input2, i.e. if there is a remainder for input1/input2. We call the function in the try block. Try block will execute if input1 is integer divisible by input2:

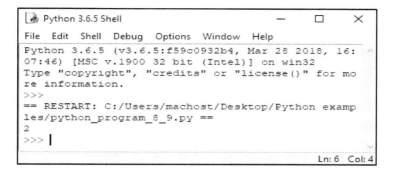

Figure 8.10. The try block is successfully executed

If input1 is not integer divisible by input2, then our custom exception will be raised:

```
def func2(input1, input2):
    if input1 % input2 !=0:
        raise  ValueError("{}  is  not  integer
divisible by {}.".format(input1, input2))
    else:
        return int(input1/input2)
try:
    print(func2(6,5))
except Exception as e:
    print(e)
```

The exception will be caught by the except keyword as follows:

```
Python 3.6.5 Shell                          —    □    ×
File  Edit  Shell  Debug  Options  Window  Help
Python 3.6.5 (v3.6.5:f59c0932b4, Mar 28 2018, 16:07:46
) [MSC v.1900 32 bit (Intel)] on win32
Type "copyright", "credits" or "license()" for more in
formation.
>>>
== RESTART: C:/Users/machost/Desktop/Python examples/p
ython_program_8_10.py ==
6 is not integer divisible by 5.
>>> |
                                              Ln: 6  Col: 4
```

Figure 8.11. Raising and catching the a exception with the raise and except blocks

That's all about the excption handling and raising in Python. Please try to solce the exercises below. After then we will start learning a very important subject in programming and Python: object-oriented programming.

8.7. Exercises

1. Write a function which accepts a dictionary and a key as its arguments. The function will return the value corresponding to the key given to it. The function will raise a custom error if the dictionary does not have the given key.

2. Use the SyntaxError exception in a simple program.

3. Write a program that imports a module. Use the exception handling mechanism to check if your program can import the module successfully (happens for existing built-in modules) or raises an exception if the module cannot be imported (happens if the program cannot find the module).

4. Use the *else* keyword in a simple exception handling program.

5. Write a program in which tries to open a text file simply by the built-in open() function. If the program opens the file successfully, print a success message. Otherwise print a custom exception message saying that the file cannot be opened.

Chapter 9. Object-Oriented Programming

9.1. Introduction to classes and objects

In programming, an *object* is the combination of related variables, methods and other data structures. Objects are derived from a concept called *class*. A class can be thought as a blueprint for producing objects belonging to this class. We can consider a car example to understand classes better. There are different cars having specific properties like colour, number of doors, brand, model year, etc. Car (as a concept) as can be considered as a class and each real car having specific properties can be thought as objects belonging to the car class. This is shown in Figure 9.1.

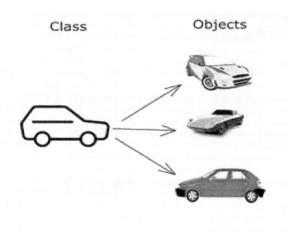

Figure 9.1. Understanding the class-object concept by an analogy

In the above figure, the class is represented as a template for producing a car. And each type of car produced using this template represents an object. Note that cars have some values and methods. For exampe, the colour and the number of doors are all values (variables) of a car while the production of this car and the movement function of the car can be considered as the methods of the car class.

9.2. Creating classes and objects in Python

Let's create a class for another popular example: the smartphone object. Similar to the car example, smartphones have different variables and methods. The variables may include its colour, weight and screen size while its methods include voice calling, video calling or connection to the Internet. We can simply define a smartphone class as follows:

```
class smartphone():
    colour = "amber"
    weight = 95
    screen_size=4.7
```

Please remember that when we define functions, they do not do anything unless we call them. Just as in functions, classes do not perform any operation unless we derive objects from them. We create objects from classes and our class definition becomes active in this way. We use the following template for deriving an object from a class:

name_of_the_derived_object = class_name()

Therefore, we can create a *smartphone1* object in the following way:

```
smartphone1 = smartphone()
```

We have now created an object. We can access its variables by using the dot notation:

name_of_the_object.variable_name

Let's print the variables of the smartphone1 object:

```
class smartphone():
    colour = "amber"
    weight = 95
    screen_size=4.7

smartphone1 = smartphone()
print("The colur variable is", smartphone1.colour)
```

```
print("The weight variable is", smartphone1.weight)
print("The     screen    size    variable    is",
smartphone1.screen_size)
```

The output of this program is as follows:

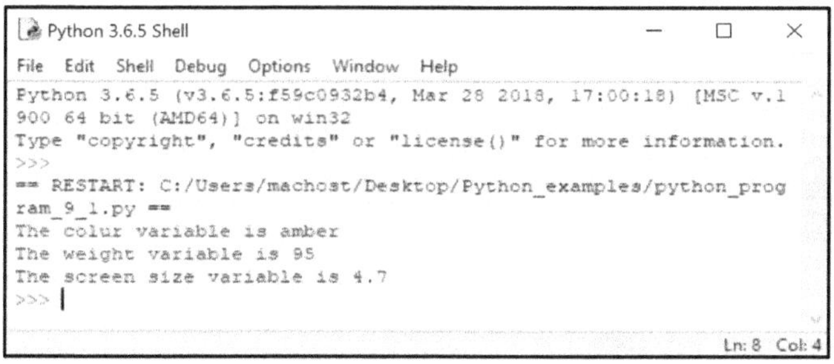

Figure 9.2. The values of the variables of the smartphone1 object is printed

We can generate another object from the same class named smartphone2 and its variables will have the same values:

```
smartphone2 = smartphone()
print("The colur variable is", smartphone2.colour)
print("The weight variable is", smartphone2.weight)
print("The     screen    size    variable    is",
smartphone2.screen_size)
```

The output will be the same:

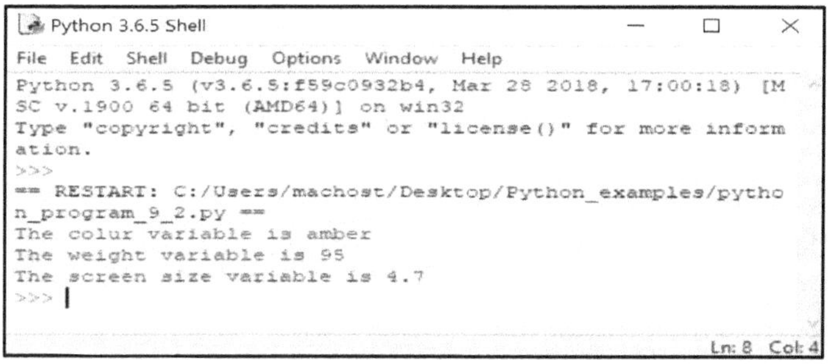

Figure 9.3. Another object derived from the same class has the variables with the same values

9.3. Changing the variables of an object

We can change the values of the variables after the object is created. Let's change the variables of the smartphone2 object:

```
smartphone2.colour="white"
smartphone.2.weight=110
```

Let's print the values of the variables of smartphone2 object again:

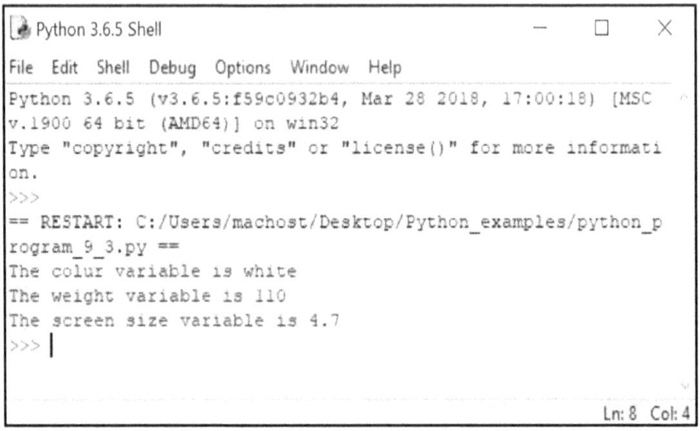

Figure 9.4. The updated variables of smartphone2 object are reprinted

9.4. The constructor method (_init_() method)

All classes in fact have a hidden constructor method called the __init__() method. When we create an object from a class, this method is automatically called. This method has no parameters by default but we can re-define this method explicitly to send parameters during object creation for setting the variables of objects at the creation time:

```
class smartphone():
    def __init__(self, colour_param, weight_param,
screen_size_param):
        self.colour=colour_param
        self.weight=weight_param
        self.screen_size=screen_size_param

smartphone3=smartphone()
```

Here, the __init__() method has the self keyword as the first parameter. This is a must for all methods and variables we refer to in a class definition. Then comes the three parameters: colour_param, weight_param and screen_size_param. The body of the __init__() method has three code lines which assign the parameters of the __init__() method to the variables of the class namely the colour, weight and screen_size variables. After the smartphone() class definition, we derive an object named *smartphone3* at the last line. Let's run this program to see its output:

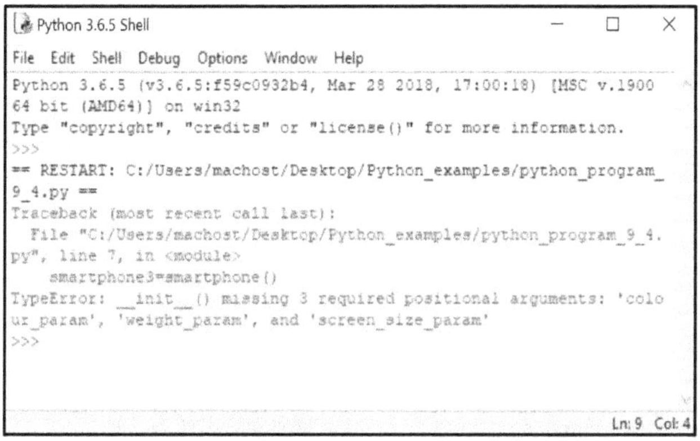

Figure 9.5. Error in the constructor method

The __init__() method issued an error and the object was not created. It is because we tried to create the smartphone3 object without any parameters however we had to give the required three parameters. We can create this object correctly as follows and print the values of these variables:

```python
class smartphone():
    def __init__(self, colour_param, weight_param,
screen_size_param):
        self.colour=colour_param
        self.weight=weight_param
        self.screen_size=screen_size_param

smartphone3=smartphone("red", 100, 4.5)  #Creating
the object

print("Colour:", smartphone3.colour)
```

```
print("Weight:", smartphone3.weight)
print("Screen size:", smartphone3.screen_size)
```

The output will print the valuef of the variablef of *smartphone3* object, which were assigned during the creation of this object:

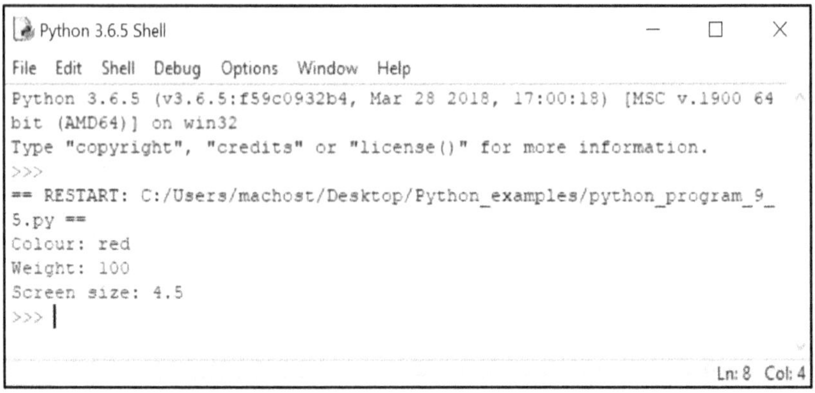

Figure 9.6. The values of the variables of *smartphone3* object

9.5. Adding custom methods to classes

We can add our own methods in a classe and these classes will be accessible in each object derived from this class. We printed the values of the variables of smartphone objects above. Let's add the a custom printing method inside the smartphone class:

```
class smartphone():
    def __init__(self, colour_param, weight_param,
screen_size_param):
        self.colour=colour_param
        self.weight=weight_param
        self.screen_size=screen_size_param

    def show_properties(self):
        print("We are inside the show_properties()
method of the current object")
        print("Colour:", self.colour)
        print("Weight:", self.weight)
        print("Screen size:", self.screen_size)
```

We have defined a custom method named show_properties. Note that it has the default *self* keyword as the parameter so that Python interpreter will know that this function refers to the current object derived from this class. Also remember that this *self* parameter is not given when executing the method (as in the __init__() method) since it is a default parameter. We accessed the variables of the current object in our method as *self.colour*, *self.weight* and *self.screen_size* expressions since we are referring to the current object.

Let's create a new smartphone4 object from this class and execute its show_properties() method. Note that the method of an object is also accessed by the dot notation:

object_name.method_name()

```
class smartphone():
    def __init__(self, colour_param, weight_param,
screen_size_param):
        self.colour=colour_param
        self.weight=weight_param
        self.screen_size=screen_size_param

    def show_properties(self):
        print("We are inside the show_properties()
method of the current object")
        print("Colour:", self.colour)
        print("Weight:", self.weight)
        print("Screen size:", self.screen_size)

smartphone4=smartphone("red", 100, 4.5) #Creating
the object

smartphone4.show_properties() #Running the object's
method
print("Colour:", smartphone3.colour)
print("Weight:", smartphone3.weight)
print("Screen size:", smartphone3.screen_size)
```

Please run this program and you can see the values of the variables of the *smartphone4* object:

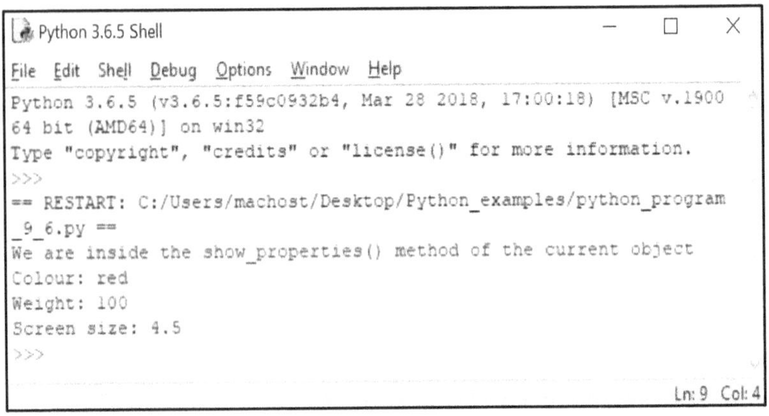

Figure 9.7. Using the method of an object

We can also use parameters in the methods of a class, and change the values of the variables, or for any other operation. Let's define a new method named change_colour() which takes the new colour as a parameter and changes the value of the colour variable of the object:

```python
class smartphone():
    def __init__(self, colour_param, weight_param,
screen_size_param):
        self.colour=colour_param
        self.weight=weight_param
        self.screen_size=screen_size_param

    def show_properties(self):
        print("We are inside the show_properties()
method of the current object.")
        print("Colour:", self.colour)
        print("Weight:", self.weight)
        print("Screen size:", self.screen_size)

    def change_colour(self, new_colour_param):
        print("The colour variable is being changed
inside the class.")
        self.colour=new_colour_param
```

Let's create a new object called smartphone5, print its variable values, apply the change_colour() method and then print the values again:

```
class smartphone():
    def __init__(self, colour_param, weight_param,
screen_size_param):
        self.colour=colour_param
        self.weight=weight_param
        self.screen_size=screen_size_param

    def show_properties(self):
        print("We are inside the show_properties()
method of the current object.")
        print("Colour:", self.colour)
        print("Weight:", self.weight)
        print("Screen size:", self.screen_size)

    def change_colour(self, new_colour_param):
        print("The colour variable is being changed
inside the class.")
        self.colour=new_colour_param

smartphone5=smartphone("red", 100, 4.5) #Creating
the object

smartphone5.show_properties() #Running the object's
method

smartphone5.change_colour("green")

smartphone5.show_properties()
```

The object will be created using the default value of "red" for the colour variable and then will be changed to "green" as shown in Figure 9.8.

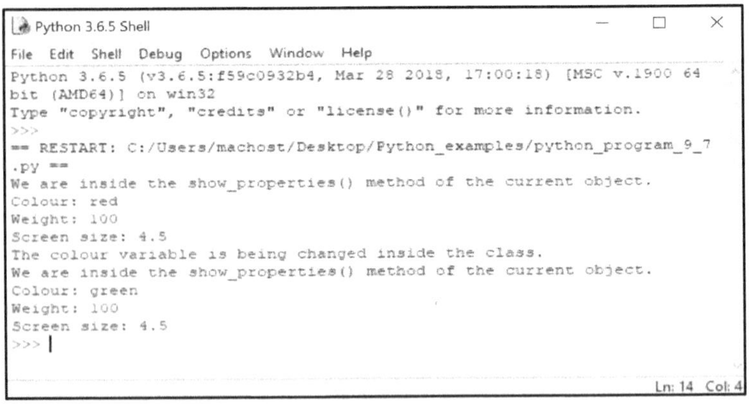

Figure 9.8. Changing the value of a variable using the change_colour() method with a parameter

9.6. Inheritance

Just as living things inherit from his/her parents, classes can also inherit from its parent classes. Thanks to the inheritance, we do not need to rewrite the contents of a parent class again and again when we are generating a new class which will include the contents of the parent class plus new things inside it. The template for inheriting from a parent class is as follows:

class child_class(name_of_the_parent_class):

    additional_contents

    to_the_parent_class

We have defined a smartphne class in the previous example. Let's now *extend* this class by creating a child class called *tablet* as follows:

```
class tablet(smartphone):
    def create_input(self, new_input):
        print("A new input is defined spesific to
            the 'tablet' class.")
        self.data_input=new_input
```

This class extends the 'smartphone' class and has an additional create_input() method. Let's now use this class in a program where we will first create a tablet object and then add a new data input to it (which is done through the create_input() method specific to this class):

```
class smartphone():
    def __init__(self, colour_param, weight_param,
screen_size_param):
        self.colour=colour_param
        self.weight=weight_param
        self.screen_size=screen_size_param

    def show_properties(self):
        print("We are inside the show_properties()
method of the current object.")
        print("Colour:", self.colour)
        print("Weight:", self.weight)
        print("Screen size:", self.screen_size)

    def change_colour(self, new_colour_param):
        print("The colour variable is being changed
inside the class.")
        self.colour=new_colour_param

class tablet(smartphone):
    def create_input(self, new_input):
        print("A new input is defined spesific to
            the 'tablet' class.")
        self.data_input=new_input

tablet1=tablet("red",   100,   4.5)   #Creating   the
object

tablet1.show_properties()   #Running   the   object's
method

tablet1.create_input("USB")

tablet1.show_properties()
print("The data input for this object is",
        tablet1.data_input)
```

The output will show the variables of the tablet1 object inherited from the 'smartphone' class plus its new variable: data_input using the last command:

```
Python 3.6.5 Shell                                          —    □    ×
File  Edit  Shell  Debug  Options  Window  Help
Python 3.6.5 (v3.6.5:f59c0932b4, Mar 28 2018, 17:00:18) [MSC v.1900 64 bit (AM
D64)] on win32
Type "copyright", "credits" or "license()" for more information.
>>>
== RESTART: C:/Users/machost/Desktop/Python_examples/python_program_9_8.py ==
We are inside the show_properties() method of the current object.
Colour: red
Weight: 100
Screen size: 4.5
A new input is defined spesific to the 'tablet' class.
We are inside the show_properties() method of the current object.
Colour: red
Weight: 100
Screen size: 4.5
The data input for this object is USB
>>>
                                                                   Ln: 15  Col: 4
```

Figure 9.9. Creating the *tablet1* object which inherits 3 of its properties from the *smartphone* class and then printing the values of its variables

A final note: If we define a new method in the child method which has the same name as a method in its parent method, then the parent's method is *overridden*. In this case, if we particularly need to use the overridden method, we can use the *super* keyword to access the parent's overridden method. These are useful information but rarely used in practice.

We have learned the basics of object-oriented programming in Python in this chapter. This is also the end of the first part of this book in which you learned the basics of Python enough to develop more advanced and practical programs in the following chapters. Please try to write the programs given in the exercises below before continuing to the next part of the book in which we will start with file operations in Python.

9.7. Exercises

1. Write a class in which you define a method to perform factorial of a given number and create an object derived from this class to calculate a factorial.

2. Write a class named Rectangle which is constructed by the width and length and has a method which calculates the perimeter of the rectangle.

3. Write a simple class of your preference and then create an object using this class. Then print the name of this class using the __name__ attribute of the class.

4. Write a simple class and create an object derived from that class. Use the type() function on that object to see how Python describes an object.

5. Find out how you can delete an object in Python.

Part II. File and Database Operations

Chapter 10. File Operations in Python

File reading and writing operations are pretty easy in Python. We utilize a file object to access the file and perform the operations accordingly.

10.1. Reading files

We use the open() function to create a file handling object. In order to open a file for reading, we use the "r" parameter in the open() function togehter with the path and the name of the file as follows:

file_handle = open("filepath\filename", "r")

Let's create a text file on our desktop (using Notepad if you're using Windows) with the following contents as an example:

Hello Python...

Programming in Pythonic way is awesome.

Please save this text file as *new.txt* on your desktop. Then in the IDLE Editor, use the open() function as follows:

```
file_object=open("C:\\Users\\username\\Desktop\\new.
txt", "r")
```

Note that username has to be replaced with your user name in Windows. Also note that we use double backslahes in the file path for preventing possible character coding errors. We will use the file_object for performing operations on this file. Let's read the file and display its contents:

```
file_object=open("C:\\Users\\machost\\Desktop\\new.
txt", "r")
print("The contents of new.txt are:")
print(file_object.read())
file_object.close()
```

We use the read() method applied to the file object: file_object.read() to read the file and then print in in Python:

```
Python 3.6.5 Shell                                    —    □    ✕
File  Edit  Shell  Debug  Options  Window  Help
Python 3.6.5 (v3.6.5:f59c0932b4, Mar 28 2018, 17:00:18) [MSC v
.1900 64 bit (AMD64)] on win32
Type "copyright", "credits" or "license()" for more informatio
n.
>>>
== RESTART: C:/Users/machost/Desktop/Python_examples/python_pr
ogram_10_1.py ==
The contents of new.txt are:
Hello Python...
Programming in Pythonic way is awesome.
>>> |
                                                        Ln: 8  Col: 4
```

Figure 10.1. Reading a file in Python

Note that we need to close a file after we have done with it, otherwise the file stays open in our program and cannot be accessed by other programs. This is not a problem with this simple example but causes problems as your programs get bigger and need to access a file from different modules of your program. We simply apply the close() operation to close a file as in the last line of the program above.

There is also a method called readline() that is used to read a single line of a file at a time as follows:

```
file_object=open("C:\\Users\\machost\\Desktop\\new.
txt", "r")
print("The contents of new.txt are:")
print(file_object.readline())
file_object.close()
```

Since we executed the readline() method only once, the first line of the file will be read:

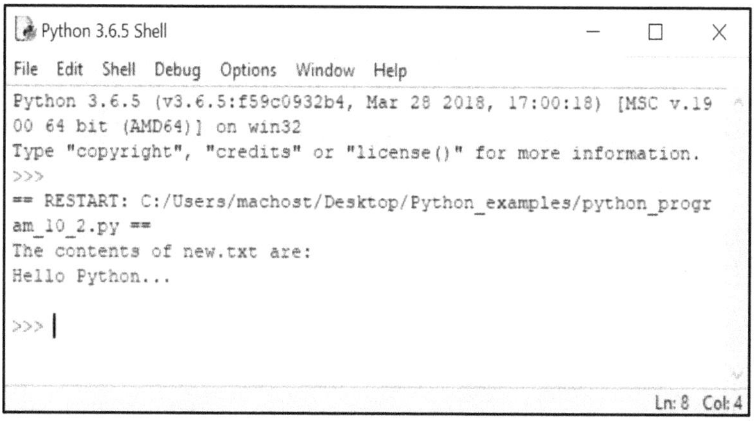

Figure 10.2. Using the readline() method (1)

We need to execute the readline() method two times to read both lines of the new.txt file:

```
file_object=open("C:\\Users\\machost\\Desktop\\new.
txt", "r")
print("The contents of new.txt are:")
print(file_object.readline())
print(file_object.readline())
file_object.close()
```

The output will have two lines of the new.txt file:

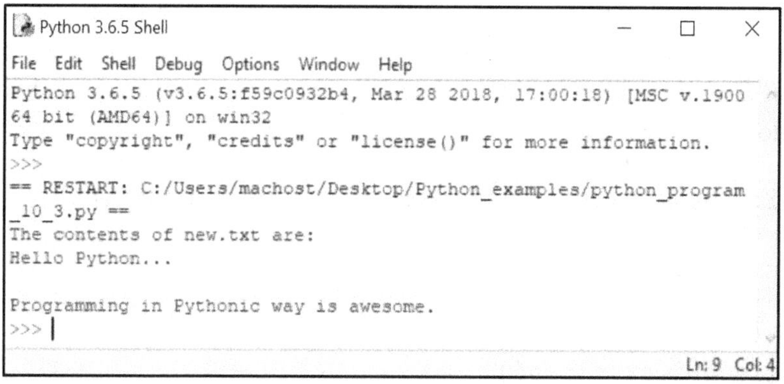

Figure 10.3. Reading multiple lines with multiple readline() methods

We also have a similar method named readlines() which returns all the lines of a file as elements of a list:

```
file_object=open("C:\\Users\\machost\\Desktop\\new.
txt", "r")
print("The contents of new.txt are:")
print(file_object.readlines())
file_object.close()
```

We are printing the list returned by the readlines() method in this program:

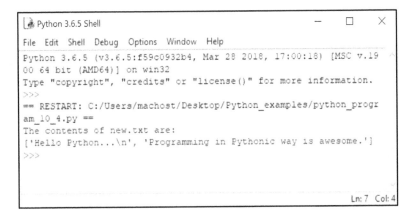

Figure 10.4. Obtaining all the lines as a list using the readlines() method

Files are read byte by byte in Python. As we call read the file, the file handler pointer is moved from the start position (0) to the last read byte. We can query the position of the file pointer by the tell() method as follows:

```
file_object=open("C:\\Users\\machost\\Desktop\\new.
txt", "r")
print("The contents of new.txt are:")
print(file_object.readline())
print(file_object.tell())
file_object.close()
```

The first line of the new.txt file is read by the file_object.readline() method which is "Hello Python..." and then the file pointer has moved to the next line by the "\n" newline command. Therefore the file pointer moved 15+2=17bytes and the tell() mtehod will exactly tell this:

```
Python 3.6.5 Shell                                    —    □    ×

File  Edit  Shell  Debug  Options  Window  Help
Python 3.6.5 (v3.6.5:f59c0932b4, Mar 28 2018, 17:00:18) [MSC v.190
0 64 bit (AMD64)] on win32
Type "copyright", "credits" or "license()" for more information.
>>>
== RESTART: C:\Users\machost\Desktop\Python_examples\python_progra
m_10_5.py ==
The contents of new.txt are:
Hello Python...

17
>>>
                                                          Ln: 4  Col: 12
```

Figure 10.5. Accessing the file pointer location by the tell() method

There is another method related to file reading called the seek() method. It takes a parameter as an integer which is the location to which we want to move the file pointer to. For example, if we apply this method as file_object.seek(3), the pointer will be moved to the 3rd byte in the file and start reading from there. Let's see it in action:

```
file_object=open("C:\\Users\\machost\\Desktop\\new.
txt", "r")
print("The contents of new.txt are:")
file_object.seek(3)
print(file_object.readline())
file_object.close()
```

The file pointer has been moved to 3rd location by the third command: file_object.seek(3) and then the curent line has been read by the file_object.readline() command. Since the first line in the new.txt file is "Hello Python...", the file pointer will be moved to the 4th character and the line will be read:

```
Python 3.6.5 Shell                                          —   □   ×
File  Edit  Shell  Debug  Options  Window  Help
Python 3.6.5 (v3.6.5:f59c0932b4, Mar 28 2018, 17:00:18) [MSC v.1900 64
bit (AMD64)] on win32
Type "copyright", "credits" or "license()" for more information.
>>>
== RESTART: C:/Users/machost/Desktop/Python_examples/python_program_10
_6.py ==
The contents of new.txt are:
lo Python...

>>> |
                                                            Ln: 8  Col: 4
```

Figure 10.6. Using the seek() method to move the file pointer

Note that, as in lists and strings, the indices of characters in a file are counted starting from zero therefore moving the pointer to the 3rd location actually moved it to the 4th character.

10.2. Creating and writing files

We can write to the files simply by opening the file with the "w" paraneter in the open() method and then using the write() method. We give the characters to be written as the parameter to this method. This method returns the number of bytes written to the file:

file_handle = open("filepath\filename", "w")

num_of_bytes=write("Text to be written")

The file is created all over when we use the "w" parameter in the open() method meaning that if the file has contents previous to these operations, they will be overwritten (lost). Let's open our new.txt file using the "w" parameter and write new text into it:

```
#1-Read file
file_object=open("C:\\Users\\machost\\Desktop\\new.
txt", "r")
print("The previous contents of new.txt are:")
print(file_object.read())
file_object.close()
```

```
#2-Write new text to file
file_object=open("C:\\Users\\machost\\Desktop\\new.
txt", "w")
bytes_written=file_object.write("New text")
print("File is rewritten. The number of written
bytes is:", bytes_written)
file_object.close()

#3-Read file again
file_object=open("C:\\Users\\machost\\Desktop\\new.
txt", "r")
print("The current contents of new.txt are:")
print(file_object.read())
file_object.close()
```

The file will be read by opening with the "r" parameter. And then the file be opened by the "w" parameter for writing on it and then read again after the writing operation. The output of this program will be as follows:

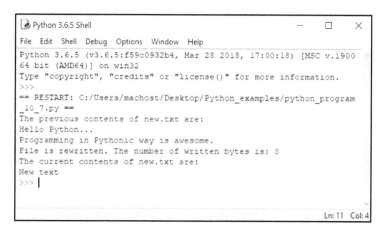

File 10.7. Rewriting a file

10.3. Modifying files

The previous contents of the file is lost when we written using the write() method in this example. It is because we have opened the file with the "w" parameter. Alternatively, we can use the "a" parameter to open the file for writing. In this case, the data we write will be appended to the file, i.e. will be added to the end of the file without erasing the previous content. The new.txt file has been modified by the previous program and has the contents of "New text" inside it. If we execute the following program, we will append the "Extra new text" to the new.txt file:

```
#1-Read file
file_object=open("C:\\Users\\machost\\Desktop\\new.
txt", "r")
print("The previous contents of new.txt are:")
print(file_object.read())
file_object.close()
```

The output of this program is as follows:

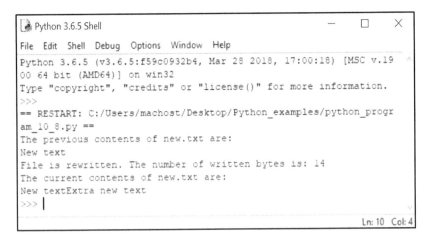

Figure 10.8. Appending data to a file

Note that, the "Extra new text" is written next to the existing data "New text". We could write the new data in the new line if we used the newline escape sequence "\n" in front of it:

```
#1-Read file
file_object=open("C:\\Users\\machost\\Desktop\\new.
txt", "r")
print("The previous contents of new.txt are:")
print(file_object.read())
```

```
file_object.close()

#2-Append new text to file
file_object=open("C:\\Users\\machost\\Desktop\\new.
txt", "a")
bytes_written=file_object.write("\nExtra extra new
text")
print("File is rewritten. The number of written
bytes is:", bytes_written)
file_object.close()

#3-Read file again
file_object=open("C:\\Users\\machost\\Desktop\\new.
txt", "r")
print("The current contents of new.txt are:")
print(file_object.read())
file_object.close()
```

The "Extra extra new text" will be appended to the new line:

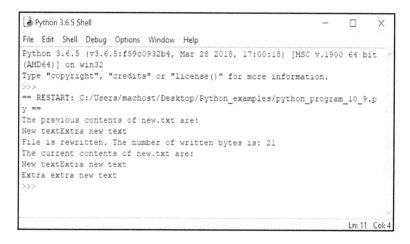

Figure 10.9. Appending new data in a new line

We can also append data to any position in a file. The steps we need to perform are 1) to open the file using the "r+" parameter (which allows both reading and writing the file), 2) use the seek() method and move the file pointer to the position we will write to and 3) use the write() method

169

as usual. For this example, I have created a new file named new2.txt with the following content:

Programming in Python is fun.

We can now open this file, move the file pointer to location 4 and append new content as follows:

```
#1-Read file
file_object=open("C:\\Users\\machost\\Desktop\\new2
.txt", "r")
print("The previous contents of new.txt are:")
print(file_object.read())
file_object.close()

#2-Append new text to file
file_object=open("C:\\Users\\machost\\Desktop\\new2
.txt", "r+")
file_object.seek(4)
bytes_written=file_object.write("New content")
print("File is rewritten. The number of written
bytes is:", bytes_written)
file_object.close()

#3-Read file again
file_object=open("C:\\Users\\machost\\Desktop\\new2
.txt", "r")
print("The current contents of new.txt are:")
print(file_object.read())
file_object.close()
```

The new data "\nNew content" will be appended to the file starting from the 5th character (which is pointed by the 4th location of the file pointer) nas shown in Figure 10.10.

We have learned the basics of file operations in Python in this chapter. Writing to files is practical if the data to be written is not complex. If the data has a complex structure, it is better to use a database as we will learn in the next chapter. Please try to write the programs given in the exercise section below before continuing to the next chapter.

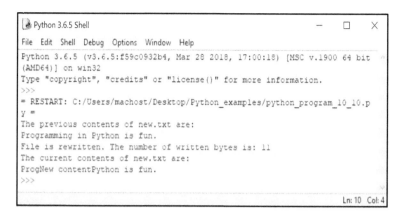

Figure 10.10. Appending data to an arbitrary location in a file using the seek() method

10.4. Exercises

1. Write a program to create a new text file and write "Hello Python" 10 times inside it.

2. Write a program to read and display the contents of the spreadsheet file.

3. Write a program to read a text file and display the number of lines inside it.

4. Write a program to delete a given line from a file.

5. Write a program to copy the contents of a text file to a newly created file.

Chapter 11. Database Operations in Python

11.1. What is a database?

Databases are files which contain structured information. The data in database can be written and queried in various ways. Data reading and writing operations are performed by using the specific command sets sent to these databases. These commands are written in the languages that are unique to the database type. Database commands can be sent via Python and other languages such as PHP therefore providing access to databases from these languages.

There are numerous database types and languages. Some databases, especially big databases, have to be installed as a program to run. On the other hand, some databases do not need to be installed and can be created and accessed as a simple file. Python has the power to work with a wide spectrum of databases however in this book we will learn using the *Sqlite* database, which do not need a server and can just be created and accessed as a simple file. Once you learn using the Sqlite database, you can generalize your knowledge easily to work with other database types. Sqlite databases are accessed via a database language set called Structured Query Language (SQL) as we will learn in this chapter.

11.2. Creating an Sqlite database

We will use the *sqlite3* library included in the Python distribution for performing database operations. We will use the following code structure to create a new Sqlite database named new_database:

```
import sqlite3 as sql

db_handle=sql.connect("new_database.db")

db_handle.close()
```

In the first line we imported the sqlite3 module as sql. And then we created a database handle object by using the connect() method with the database name as its parameter. Then we closed the database connection with the close() method in the last line. Please note the similarity with the file creating and closing operations we learned in the previous chapter. Let's run this program and we will have a database file named new_database.db in the same folder with our Python file:

```
Python 3.6.5 Shell                                    —    □    ×

File  Edit  Shell  Debug  Options  Window  Help

Python 3.6.5 (v3.6.5:f59c0932b4, Mar 28 2018, 17:00:18) [MSC
v.1900 64 bit (AMD64)] on win32
Type "copyright", "credits" or "license()" for more informati
on.
>>>
== RESTART: C:\Users\machost\Desktop\Python_examples\python_p
rogram_11_1.py ==
>>>

                                                          Ln: 5  Col: 4
```

Figure 11.1. Our first database program is executed

Note that this program does not have any output in the command prompt (and no error!). But we have the database file created in the same directory:

new_database	28.06.2018 06:39	Data Base File
python_program_11_2	28.06.2018 06:39	PY Dosyası
python_program_11_1	28.06.2018 06:34	PY Dosyası
python_program_10_10	26.06.2018 08:38	PY Dosyası
python_program_10_9	26.06.2018 08:20	PY Dosyası
python_program_10_8	26.06.2018 08:16	PY Dosyası
python_program_10_7	26.06.2018 08:06	PY Dosyası
python_program_10_6	26.06.2018 07:22	PY Dosyası

Figure 11.2. The Sqlite database file has been created by our program

If we execute our program once again, a new database file will not be created, but we will have just made a connection to the existing database file.

11.3. Adding a table to the database

We have now created an Sqlite database. Sqlite databases contain data tables inside each of which contains their specific properties. In other words, an Sqlite database typically contains several tables and each table contains several data properties. Therefore, we first need to create a table structure in an Sqlite database file first and then we can add data to this table. Let's create a table in our new_database.db file called CAR in which we will later write (insert) data related to cars. We can use the following program to create a new table in our database file:

```python
import sqlite3 as sql

db_handle=sql.connect("new_database.db")

cursor=db_handle.cursor()

cursor.execute("CREATE TABLE CARS(COLOUR TEXT, YEAR INT, NUM_OF_DOORS INT)")

db_handle.commit()

db_handle.close()
```

In the third line we created a cursor object which is used to access the database to run SQL commands. In the next line, we execute an SQL command with the execute() method applied on the cursor object. The SQL command is given as the parameter string to the execute() method. The SQL command we use here is:

```
"CREATE    TABLE    CARS(COLOUR    TEXT,    YEAR    INT,
NUM_OF_DOORS INT)"
```

Which means "create a table named CARS with the columns named COLOUR, YEAR and NUM_OF_DOORS and the data type these tables may have are TEXT (string), INT (integer) and INT, respectively".

In the next command, we use the commit() method on the database handle which makes changes to the database file according to previously given SQL commands. And finally, the database is closed in the last line. Let's execute this program:

```
Python 3.6.5 Shell                                        —    □    ×
File  Edit  Shell  Debug  Options  Window  Help
Python 3.6.5 (v3.6.5:f59c0932b4, Mar 28 2018, 17:00:18) [MSC v.1900 64 bi
t (AMD64)] on win32
Type "copyright", "credits" or "license()" for more information.
>>>
== RESTART: C:\Users\machost\Desktop\Python_examples\python_program_11_2.
py ==
>>> |




                                                              Ln: 5  Col: 4
```

Figure 11.3. Executing the table adding program doesn't produce any output in the IDLE prompt

The output doesn't have any information again. We need to view the contents of the database file, but how? We cannot view its contents by a text editor or a similar program. We need to use specific programs used for viewing databases. There are various free and paid software for this aim. We can simply use a program called SQLite Studio, which is open source and free and can be downloaded from https://sqlitestudio.pl/index.rvt?act=download. (Please perform your own virus scan as usual, as I cannot be held responsible for the contents of external links.) We can easiy download SQLite Studio and install it the Next, Next procedure. After installing, please run the SQLite Studio and you'll be presented by the following window:

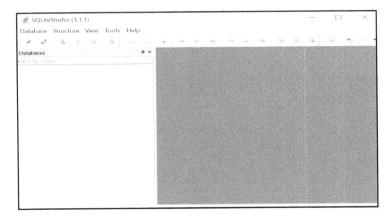

Figure 11.4. The SQLite Studio program

In order to open our database file, please navigate to Database → Add New Database in the program and select the database file as swhon in Figures 11.5, 11.6 and 11.7. Our database file will be shown in the left menu as shown in Figure 11.8.

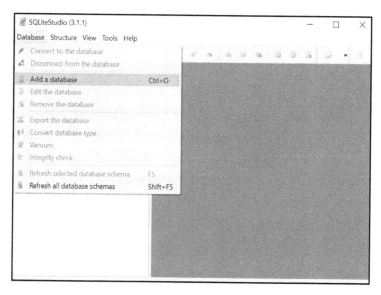

Figure 11.5. Adding a database to SQLite Studio

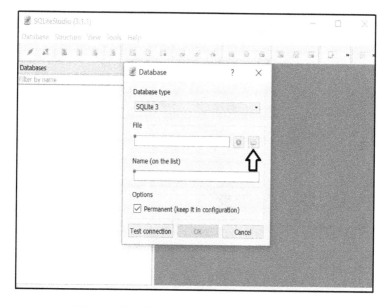

Figure 11.6. Selecting our database file (1)

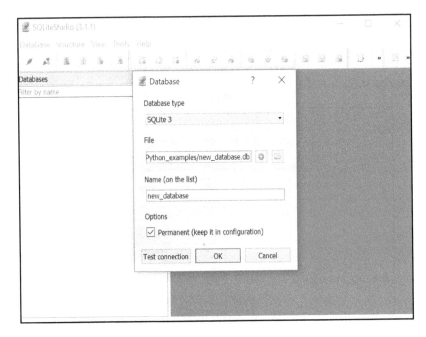

Figure 11.7. Selecting our database file (2)

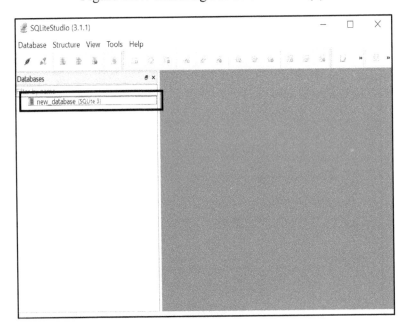

Figure 11.8. The database file is now added to the SQLite Studio program

We can now double-click on the new_database on the left menu and then its structure will be opened as shown in Figure 11.9.

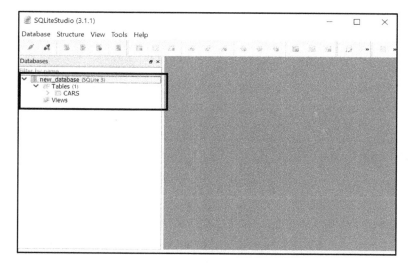

Figure 11.9. Opening the table structure of the database file

And finally, please double-click the CARS table in the left menu to view its contents in the main pane of the program as in Figure 11.10.

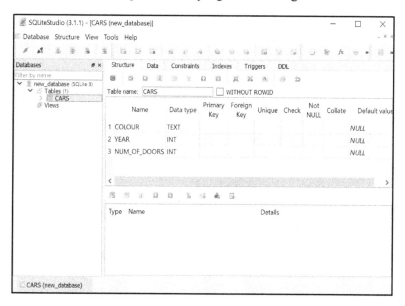

Figure 11.10. The structure of the CARS table of our new_database.db file

As you can see in the main pane, the structure of the CARS table is shown as having three rows with names of COLOUR, YEAR and NUM_OF_DOORS with the data types of TEXT, INT and INT, respectively, the same as we have given in the SQL command in our Python file when we created this table. We can now insert data to this table, again by using the SQL command in Python.

11.4. Inserting data to the table in the database

The SQL command for adding data to a table in a database is INSERT. The template for adding data in SQL is:

"INSERT INTO *TABLE_NAME* VALUES(x, y, z)"

In this format, we add the data x, y and z to the table named *TABLE_NAME*. Let's write a program to insert data to our already existing new_database.db. The CARS table in our database accepts data in the text, int and int formats, respectively. We can construct a while loop and ask for data from the user until the user enters 'q' to quit the data entry process (as we learned in the loops chapter):

```python
import sqlite3 as sql

db_handle=sql.connect("new_database.db")

cursor=db_handle.cursor()

while True:
    colour_inp=input("Please enter the colour of
                        the car ('q' to quit):")
    if colour_inp == "q":
        break
    else:
        year_inp=input("Please enter the year
                        info:")
        num_of_doors_inp=input("Please enter the
                                number of doors:")
        cursor.execute("INSERT INTO CARS
                        VALUES(?,?,?)", \
                        (colour_inp, int(year_inp),
                        int(num_of_doors_inp)))
        db_handle.commit()
```

```
db_handle.close()
```

In this program, we take the colour, year and number of doors variables from the user inside the while loop. If the user enters 'q' for the colour, the while loop breaks and the program ends. Else, the user continues to enter the year and num_of_doors inputs. We execute the SQL stataement for inserting data in the cursor.execute() method as we did previously. Then, we use the commit() method for actually applying the SQL command on the database. The SQL statement is the following:

```
"INSERT INTO CARS VALUES(?,?,?)", \(colour_inp,

int(year_inp),int(num_of_doors_inp)))
```

In this command, we use the (?,?,?) structure and assign the variables from the tuple given after the comma (colour_inp, int(year_inp),int(num_of_doors_inp)). Please note that the backslash (\) is used for continuing to break the code line to multiple lines in Python and doesn't have anything special with the SQL command. Let's execute this program and enter some data into our database:

```
Python 3.6.5 Shell                                    —    □    ×

File  Edit  Shell  Debug  Options  Window  Help
Python 3.6.5 (v3.6.5:f59c0932b4, Mar 28 2018, 17:00:18) [MSC v.1900 64
bit (AMD64)] on win32
Type "copyright", "credits" or "license()" for more information.
>>>
== RESTART: C:/Users/machost/Desktop/Python_examples/python_program_11
_3.py ==
Please enter the colour of the car ('q' to quit):red
Please enter the year info:2012
Please enter the number of doors:4
Please enter the colour of the car ('q' to quit):black
Please enter the year info:2010
Please enter the number of doors:3
Please enter the colour of the car ('q' to quit):q
>>>

                                                        Ln: 12  Col: 4
```

Figure 11.11. Entering data to the database in Python

We can use the Sqlite Studio program to see if we could actually enter these data. Simply double-click the CARS table in the left hand menu of the Sqlite Studio and then click the Data tab as shown below:

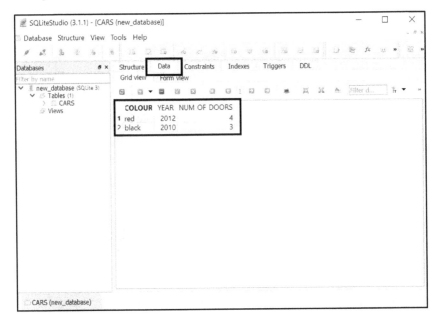

Figure 11.11. Viewing the data in the Sqlite Studio program

As we can see from this program, we entered the data properly into the database. We will see how we can read this data in the next section.

11.5. Reading data from the database

We use the SELECT command for selecting (reading by criteria) from a database. We have inserted data to the CARS table of our database above. We can read the whole data by selecting all the entries as follows:

```
import sqlite3 as sql

db_handle=sql.connect("new_database.db")

cursor=db_handle.cursor()

cursor.execute("SELECT * FROM CARS")

whole_data=cursor.fetchall()
```

```
db_handle.commit()

print(whole_data)

db_handle.close()
```

We used the SELECT * FROM CARS to select all data from the CARS table. Then we used the fetchall() method on the cursor object for taking the data and then printed the whole data:

```
Python 3.6.5 Shell                                      —    □    ✕

File  Edit  Shell  Debug  Options  Window  Help
Python 3.6.5 (v3.6.5:f59c0932b4, Mar 28 2018, 17:00:18) [MSC
v.1900 64 bit (AMD64)] on win32
Type "copyright", "credits" or "license()" for more informati
on.
>>>
== RESTART: C:/Users/machost/Desktop/Python_examples/python_p
rogram_11_4.py ==
[('red', 2012, 4), ('black', 2010, 3)]
>>>

                                                       Ln: 6  Col: 4
```

Figure 11.13. Reading all data from the CARS table

The output is a list of tuples as shown above. We can also select data according to some criteria. Let's try to select data whose colour is red. We simply use the following SQL format:

*"SELECT * FROM CARS WHERE COLOUR='red'"*

Please note the usage of single and double quotes. We cannot use double quotes inside double quotes therefore we used single quotes for the expression of the *red* string. Our program will be:

```
import sqlite3 as sql

db_handle=sql.connect("new_database.db")
```

```
cursor=db_handle.cursor()

cursor.execute("SELECT    *    FROM    CARS    WHERE
COLOUR='red'")

whole_data=cursor.fetchall()

db_handle.commit()

print(whole_data)

db_handle.close()
```

The output is the data which satisfies the criterion COLOUR='red':

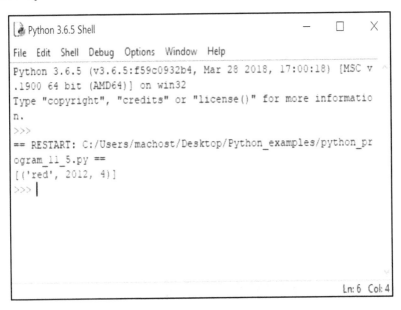

Figure 11.14. Selecting the data with COLOUR='red'

You can refer to the various websites on the Internet for seting up more advanced selecting criteria in SQL in case you need such as http://www.sqlcommands.net/.

11.6. Updating data in the database

We simply use the UPDATE command for updating data. We need to select a data set according to some criteria for updating it. For example, assume that we need to change the colour property of the data which has the year property set as 2010. We use the following SQL command for this:

UPDATE CARS SET COLOUR='white' WHERE YEAR=2010

This command means: select the data with year=2010 and update their colur as "white". We perform this in Python as follows:

```
import sqlite3 as sql

db_handle=sql.connect("new_database.db")

cursor=db_handle.cursor()

cursor.execute("UPDATE    CARS    SET    COLOUR='white'
WHERE YEAR=2010")

whole_data=cursor.fetchall()

db_handle.commit()

print(whole_data)

db_handle.close()
```

The output of the program will not give any information after execution. We need to read the database in either Python or by using the Sqlite Studio program. Let's view our table in Sqlite Studio after executing this program as in Figure 11.15.

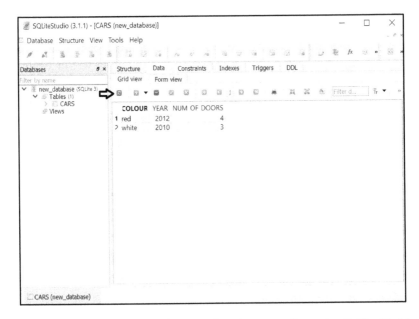

Figure 11.15. The data has been updated as seen from the Sqlite Stuido

Please note that you may need to click the update button in Sqlite Studio for viewing the updated data. The update button is shown by the arrow in Figure 11.15.

11.7. Deleting data from the database

The DELETE command enables to delete the entry(ies) from the database. However, we need to select data according to some criteria for deleting as follows

DELETE FROM TABLE_NAME WHERE CRITERIA

Let's delete the entries whose colour is "red":

```
import sqlite3 as sql

db_handle=sql.connect("new_database.db")

cursor=db_handle.cursor()

cursor.execute("DELETE     FROM     CARS     WHERE
COLOUR='red'")
```

```
db_handle.commit()

db_handle.close()
```

This program will not produce any output in the IDLE prompt but will perform the delete operation on the database. Let's view our database in the Sqlite Studio program after executing this program. It will be displayed as in Figure 11.16.

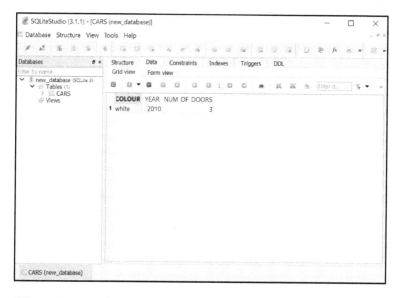

Figure 11.16. The CARS table of our database after the deletion operation.

These are the frequently used operations in SQLite databases. We will have exercises on database operations before continuing to the next chapter (and the next part) of the book where we will learn building graphical user interfaces for our Python programs.

11.8. Exercises

Note: Please view the results of your operations in the Sqlite Studio program in each of the exercises for spotting possible errors easily.

1. Write a program for creating an Sqlite database staff.db that contains a table called MAIN with the properties (fields) of NAME, SURNAME, AGE and SALARY.

2. Write a program in which the user will enter data to the MAIN table in a while loop (the program will quit if the user enters 'quit' for the NAME property).

3. Write a program to create a new table called BACKUP in the staff.db database with the same fields as the MAIN table and copy all the entries of the MAIN table to the BACKUP table automatically.

4. Write a program that will add a field called ID to both the MAIN and BACKUP tables.

5. Write a program that will assign random numbers between 100 and 1000 to the ID fields of the MAIN table. Then copy the generated IDs to the BACKUP table.

Part III. Numerical Operations and Plotting in Python

Chapter 12. Numerical Operations in Python – the *numpy* library

12.1. Introduction to *numpy*

Python is a very versatile general purpose programming language as we have learned in the previous chapters. In addition, Python also becomes a very powerful scientific programming environment with the help of some numerical libraries. These libraries are numpy (Numerical Python), scipy (Scientific Python) and matplotlib. Numpy enables us to perform matrix operations very easily and swiftly in Python. On the other hand, scipy is a more general library that contains the functionality of numpy in addition to more advanced features such as numerical differentiation and artificiall intelligence functions. matplotlib can also be thought as a part of the scientific computing environment and it provides plotting functionality both in 2D and 3D. We will study numpy and matplotlib in this part of the book, leaving the scipy library to the interested reader.

12.2. Installing *numpy*

The *numpy* library is not a default built-in package. We need to install it over the Internet. We will use a package management system called pip that is built-in the Python installation (actually we have already installed pip system when we installed Python in chapter 2). For executing the pip system, open the Powershell prompt (not the IDLE prompt) as an administrator. For this, right-click on the Windows symbol at the bottom left on the screen and select Windows PowerShell (Admin) as shown below:

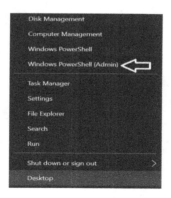

Figure 12.1. Opening the PowerShell as an administrator

The PowerShell will appear as in Figure 12.2. We execute commands in the PowerShell for making changes on our computer.

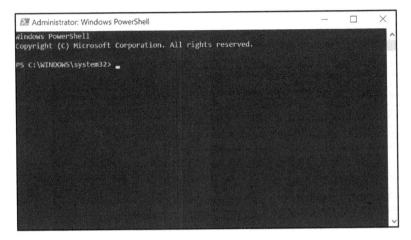

Figure 12.2. The PowerShell window

We will execute the pip program in the PowerShell for installing nmpy library. We will first navigate to the Scripts folder of our Python installation. My Python folder is C:\Python37\ for now therefore I'll go to C:\Python37\Scripts for the pip program. We can write

cd C:\Python37\Scripts

In the PowerShell and then press Enter on the keyboard. The current working folder will be changed accordingly:

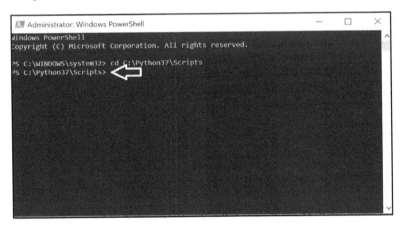

Figure 12.3. Changing the working directory in PowerShell

Now, we will execute the following command for installing numpy library in Python:

.\pip install numpy

The numpy library will be installed in the Python folder after a short time (note that this operation needs Internet for downloading the numpy installer):

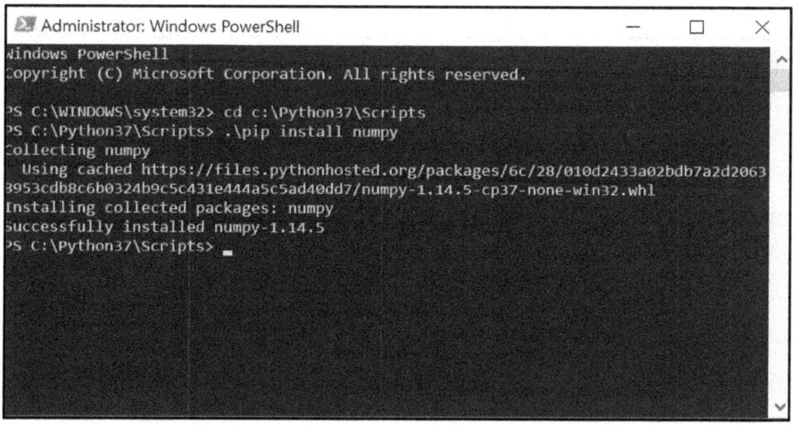

Figure 12.4. Installing numpy in the PowerShell

We are now ready for learning numpy by applications.

12.2. Creating *numpy* arrays

The first step in using numpy is creating arrays and matrices. There are numerous ways to create these structures. One way is to use predefined values as follows:

```
import numpy as np

vector1=np.array([2,4,6])
print("vector1:", vector1)
```

In the first line we imported the numpy library as np. And then we created an array called vector1 with the elements of 2, 4 and 6. And finally we print the contents of vector1:

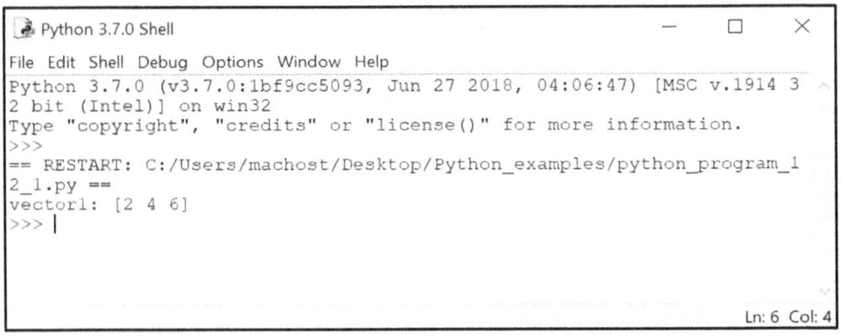

Figure 12.5. Printing a numpy array

Please note that the type of vector1 is a numpy array, not an ordinary list. We can see this by the type() function:

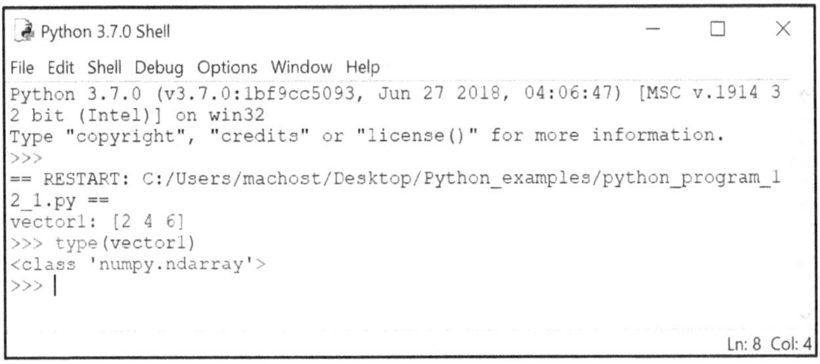

Figure 12.6. The type of vector1 is numpy array

The numpy array vector1 is a 1-dimensional array. We can also construct multidimensional arrays (matrices) as follows:

```
import numpy as np

vector2=np.array([[2,4,6], [1,2,3], [0,1,0]])
print("vector2:\n", vector2)
```

In this examplei vector2 is defined as a matrix as shown in Figure 12.7.

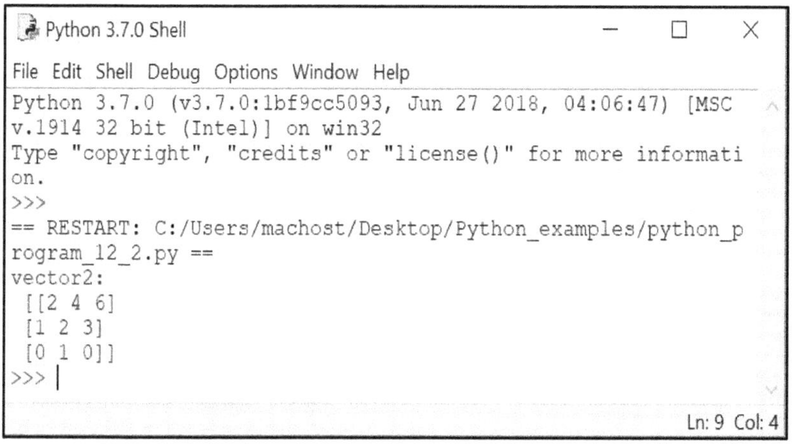

```
Python 3.7.0 Shell                                    —    □    ✕
File  Edit  Shell  Debug  Options  Window  Help
Python 3.7.0 (v3.7.0:1bf9cc5093, Jun 27 2018, 04:06:47) [MSC
v.1914 32 bit (Intel)] on win32
Type "copyright", "credits" or "license()" for more informati
on.
>>>
== RESTART: C:/Users/machost/Desktop/Python_examples/python_p
rogram_12_2.py ==
vector2:
 [[2 4 6]
 [1 2 3]
 [0 1 0]]
>>>
                                                      Ln: 9 Col: 4
```

Figure 12.7. Declaring a matrix in numpy

All-zeros, all-ones and eye matrices are also frequently used in computational solutions. numpy has built-in methods for building these matrices:

```
import numpy as np

matrix1=np.zeros((3,3)) #Declaring an all-zeros 3x3
matrix

matrix2=np.ones((4,4)) #Declaring an all-ones 4x4
matrix

matrix3=np.eye(3) #Declaring a 3x3 eye matrix

print("matrix1\n:", matrix1)
print("matrix2:\n", matrix2)
print("matrix3:\n", matrix3)
```

The matrices will be created as shown in Figure 12.8.

```
Python 3.7.0 Shell                                    —    □    ✕

File  Edit  Shell  Debug  Options  Window  Help
Python 3.7.0 (v3.7.0:1bf9cc5093, Jun 27 2018, 04:06:47) [MSC v.1
914 32 bit (Intel)] on win32
Type "copyright", "credits" or "license()" for more information.
>>>
== RESTART: C:/Users/machost/Desktop/Python_examples/python_prog
ram_12_3.py ==
matrix1
: [[0. 0. 0.]
 [0. 0. 0.]
 [0. 0. 0.]]
matrix2:
 [[1. 1. 1. 1.]
 [1. 1. 1. 1.]
 [1. 1. 1. 1.]
 [1. 1. 1. 1.]]
matrix3:
 [[1. 0. 0.]
 [0. 1. 0.]
 [0. 0. 1.]]
>>> |
                                                          Ln: 18  Col: 4
```

Figure 12.8. Creating matrices using the built-in methods in numpy

We can also create vectors and matrices using the arange() and linspace() methods when we need elements with a predefined order. The usage of the range() method is similar to the usual range() method we learned during our study on the loops. We give the start, stop and step values to the arange() method as follows:

```
import numpy as np

vector2=np.arange(0,10,2)

print("vector2:\n", vector2)
```

The vector2 array will have the values shown in Figure 12.9.

```
Python 3.7.0 Shell                                    —    □    ×

File  Edit  Shell  Debug  Options  Window  Help
Python 3.7.0 (v3.7.0:1bf9cc5093, Jun 27 2018, 04:06:47) [MSC v.19
14 32 bit (Intel)] on win32
Type "copyright", "credits" or "license()" for more information.
>>>
== RESTART: C:/Users/machost/Desktop/Python_examples/python_progr
am_12_4.py ==
vector2:
 [0 2 4 6 8]
>>> |

                                                      Ln: 7  Col: 4
```

Figure 12.9. Creating a vector using the arange() method

Note that the stop value (10) is not included in the array, similar to the range() function. The arange() method is useful if we need to enter the the step amount. However, if we are to enter the number of the array, we can use the linspace() method by specifying the number of elements instead of the step size as follows:

```
import numpy as np

vector3=np.linspace(0,20,11)

print("vector3:\n", vector3)
```

The resulting vector will have 11 elements which divide the numbers between 0 and 20 equally:

```
Python 3.7.0 Shell                                    —    □    ×

File  Edit  Shell  Debug  Options  Window  Help
Python 3.7.0 (v3.7.0:1bf9cc5093, Jun 27 2018, 04:06:47) [MSC v.1
914 32 bit (Intel)] on win32
Type "copyright", "credits" or "license()" for more information.
>>>
== RESTART: C:/Users/machost/Desktop/Python_examples/python_prog
ram_12_5.py ==
vector3:
 [ 0.  2.  4.  6.  8. 10. 12. 14. 16. 18. 20.]
>>> |

                                                      Ln: 7  Col: 4
```

Figure 12.10. Creating an array using linspace() method

We can also use the rand() method for creating vectors and matrices with random values as follows:

```
import numpy as np

vector4=np.random.rand(4)
matrix4=np.random.rand(3,3)

print("vector4:\n", vector4)
print("matrix4:\n", matrix4)
```

We create a vector with 3 random elements and a 4x4 matrix with random elements in this program:

```
Python 3.7.0 Shell                                    —    □    ✕
File Edit Shell Debug Options Window Help
Python 3.7.0 (v3.7.0:1bf9cc5093, Jun 27 2018, 04:06:47) [MSC v.1
914 32 bit (Intel)] on win32
Type "copyright", "credits" or "license()" for more information.
>>>
== RESTART: C:/Users/machost/Desktop/Python_examples/python_prog
ram_12_6.py ==
vector4:
 [0.18957953 0.1330579  0.50251711 0.14882786]
matrix4:
 [[0.07469085 0.56164976 0.57437251]
 [0.63806581 0.1781613  0.70359609]
 [0.06480387 0.17036099 0.85402159]]
>>> |
                                                      Ln: 11 Col: 4
```

Figure 12.11. Creating vectors and matrices using the rand() method

The elements of the random matrix are of float type ans between 0 and 1 by default. We can change these defaults by using different methods. For example, we can use the randn() method for generating random values between 0 and a specified number as follows:

```
import numpy as np

vector5=np.random.randint(2,200,5)

print("vector5:\n", vector5)
```

We generate a 5-element vector whose elements have the random values in the range 2-200:

```
Python 3.7.0 Shell                                    —    □    ×
File  Edit  Shell  Debug  Options  Window  Help
Python 3.7.0 (v3.7.0:1bf9cc5093, Jun 27 2018, 04:06:47) [MSC
v.1914 32 bit (Intel)] on win32
Type "copyright", "credits" or "license()" for more informat
ion.
>>>
== RESTART: C:/Users/machost/Desktop/Python_examples/python_
program_12_7.py ==
vector5:
 [117  78 177  40 134]
>>> |

                                                        Ln: 7  Col: 4
```

Figure 12.12. Generating a vector with random integers using the randint() method

Another frequently used method in numpy arrays is the reshape() method. This method re-organizes the data of the array it is applied to, according to the given parameter(s). For example, let's create a numpy array with 10 elements and reshape it to obtain a 2x5 matrix:

```
import numpy as np

vector6=np.random.randint(0,20,10)
matrix6=vector6.reshape(2,5)

print("vector6:\n", vector6)
print("matrix6:\n", matrix6)
```

The vector and the matrix obtained by reshaping this vector is printed by the program:

```
Python 3.7.0 Shell                                        —    □    ✕
File  Edit  Shell  Debug  Options  Window  Help
Python 3.7.0 (v3.7.0:1bf9cc5093, Jun 27 2018, 04:06:47) [MSC v.1914 32 bit
(Intel)] on win32
Type "copyright", "credits" or "license()" for more information.
>>>
== RESTART: C:/Users/machost/Desktop/Python_examples/python_program_12_8.py
==
vector6:
 [ 5 16  5  4 10  9 18 18 19 16]
matrix6:
 [[ 5 16  5  4 10]
  [ 9 18 18 19 16]]
>>>
                                                          Ln: 10  Col: 4
```

Figure 12.13. Reshaping a vector to obtain a matrix

Finally, we will use the min(), max() and average() methods on numpy arrays. The min() and max() methods return the minimum and maximum values of the elements of a vector or a matrix while the average() method returns the average value of these elements. Let's apply these methods on a random vector as follows:

```
import numpy as np

vector7=np.random.randint(0,20,10)

print("The  minimum  element  of  vector  7  is",
vector6.min())
print("The  maximum  element  of  vector7  is",
vector7.max())
print("The average value of the elements of vector7
is", np.average(vector7))
```

Please note that min() and max() methods are applied on the vector itself while the average() method accepts the vector under consideration. The output of this program is as in Figure 12.14.

```
Python 3.7.0 Shell                              —    □    ×
File  Edit  Shell  Debug  Options  Window  Help
Python 3.7.0 (v3.7.0:1bf9cc5093, Jun 27 2018, 04:06:47) [MSC v.1914 32
bit (Intel)] on win32
Type "copyright", "credits" or "license()" for more information.
>>>
== RESTART: C:/Users/machost/Desktop/Python_examples/python_program_12
_9.py ==
vector7 is [12  6 14 15  5  6 17 19  5 15]
The minimum element of vector 7 is 5
The maximum element of vector7 is 19
The average value of the elements of vector7 is 11.4
>>> |
                                                      Ln: 9 Col: 4
```

Figure 12.14. Using the min(), max() and average() methods on a random vector

12.3. Accessing array elements

We will firstly learn indexing numpy arrays. The indexing of arrays are similar to indexing of lists, the index of 1-D arrays start with zero and increment by one. Let's define an array and print its first element (the element with index=0):

```
import numpy as np
array1=np.array([1,3,5,7,9])
print("array1[0]=", array1[0])
```

The first element will be printed:

```
Python 3.7.0 Shell                              —    □    ×
File  Edit  Shell  Debug  Options  Window  Help
Python 3.7.0 (v3.7.0:1bf9cc5093, Jun 27 2018, 04:06:47) [MS
C v.1914 32 bit (Intel)] on win32
Type "copyright", "credits" or "license()" for more informa
tion.
>>>
= RESTART: C:/Users/machost/Desktop/Python_examples/python_
program_12_10.py =
array1[0]= 1
>>> |
                                                      Ln: 6 Col: 4
```

Figure 12.15. Printing the first element of a numpy array

Can you guess the element with index 4?

```
print("array1[4]=", array1[4])
```

It is the 5th element:

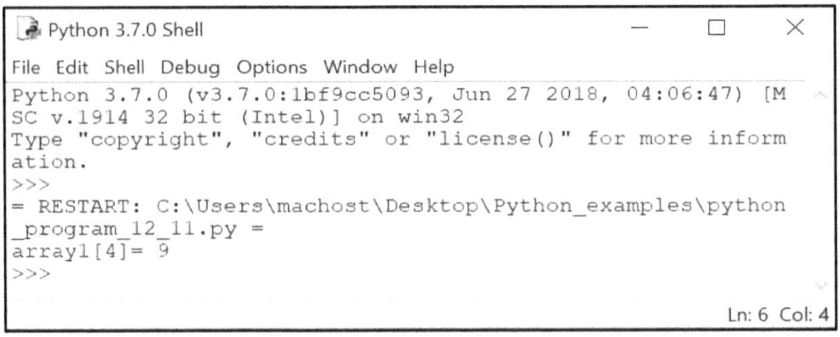

Figure 12.16. Printing the fifth element (index=4)

We can teka a portion of the array using the semicolon as in lists. Let's create a longer array and then print its element from index=2 and index=10:

```
import numpy as np
array2=np.arange(1,20,2)
print("array2=", array2)
print("array2[2:9]=",array2[2:9])
```

The array and its portion is printed as follows:

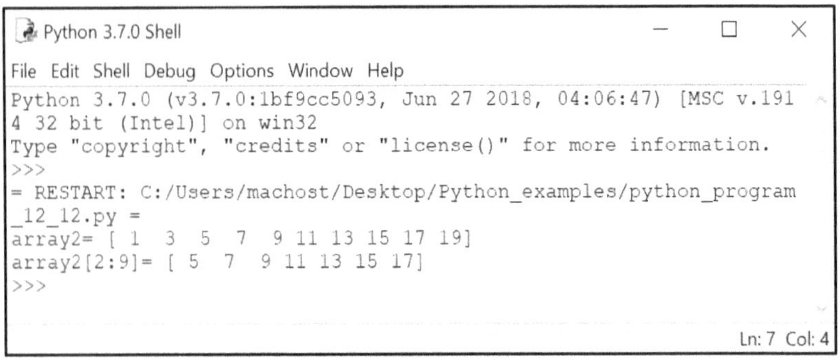

Figure 12.17. Taking a portion of a numpy array

Please note that the starting index is included (index=2) but the end index (index=9) is not included.

Indexing of 2-D arrays (matrices) is a bit different than the indexing of 2-D lists. We use double square quotes to refer to individual elements of a matrix as follows:

```
import numpy as np
matrix1=np.array([[1,2,3], [4,5,6], [7,8,9]])
print("matrix1=\n", matrix1)
print("matrix1[1][1]=\n", matrix1[1][1])
print("matrix1[0][2]=\n", matrix1[0][2])
```

The matrix is as follows:

$$matrix\,1 = \begin{bmatrix} 1 & 2 & 3 \\ 4 & 5 & 6 \\ 7 & 8 & 9 \end{bmatrix}$$

The expression matrix1[1][1] accesses the element in the second row and the second coloumn therefore the result is 5. The next expression is matrix1[0][2] which refers to the first row and the third coloumn therefore the value of 3:

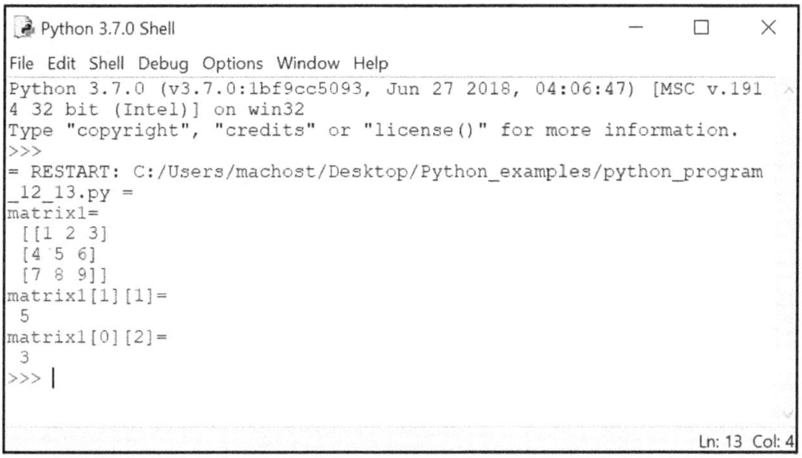

Figure 12.18. Accessing the elements of a 2-D array

We can access these elements by using the format *2D_array[row, coloumn]*:

```
import numpy as np
matrix1=np.array([[1,2,3], [4,5,6], [7,8,9]])
print("matrix1=\n", matrix1)
print("matrix1[1, 1]=\n", matrix1[1, 1])
print("matrix1[0, 2]=\n", matrix1[0, 2])
```

```
Python 3.7.0 Shell                                    —    □    ✕

File  Edit  Shell  Debug  Options  Window  Help
Python 3.7.0 (v3.7.0:1bf9cc5093, Jun 27 2018, 04:06:47) [MSC v.1914 3
2 bit (Intel)] on win32
Type "copyright", "credits" or "license()" for more information.
>>>
= RESTART: C:/Users/machost/Desktop/Python_examples/python_program_12
_14.py =
matrix1=
 [[1 2 3]
 [4 5 6]
 [7 8 9]]
matrix1[1, 1]=
 5
matrix1[0, 2]=
 3
>>>
                                                          Ln: 13 Col: 4
```

Figure 12.19. Accessing the matrix elements using the [row, coloumn] format

12.4. Elementwise operations on arrays

We usually need to perform elementwise operations on array elements and fortunately this is very easy in Python. For example, let's define two 1-D arrays (vectors) and add them:

```
import numpy as np
x=np.array([1,3,5,6,7])
y=np.array([2,4,5,5,0])
z=x+y
print("x=", x)
print("y=", y)
print("z=", z)
```

The elements of z will be the individual sums of the elements of x and y:

```
Python 3.7.0 Shell                                    —    □    ×
File Edit Shell Debug Options Window Help
Python 3.7.0 (v3.7.0:1bf9cc5093, Jun 27 2018, 04:06:47) [MSC v.19
14 32 bit (Intel)] on win32
Type "copyright", "credits" or "license()" for more information.
>>>
= RESTART: C:/Users/machost/Desktop/Python_examples/python_progra
m_12_15.py =
x= [1 3 5 6 7]
y= [2 4 5 5 0]
z= [ 3  7 10 11  7]
>>>
                                                        Ln: 8 Col: 4
```

Figure 12.20. Adding two arrays

Similarly we can also do other operations like subtraction, multiplication and division:

```
import numpy as np
x=np.array([1,3,5,6,7])
y=np.array([2,4,5,5,0])
z=x+y
print("x=", x)
print("y=", y)
print("x-y=",x-y)
print("x*y=", x*y)
print("x/y=", x/y)
```

The output will tell that Python encountered a division by zero (since the last element of y is zero) but will show it as Inf meaning Infinite:

```
Python 3.7.0 Shell                                    —    □    ×
File Edit Shell Debug Options Window Help
Python 3.7.0 (v3.7.0:1bf9cc5093, Jun 27 2018, 04:06:47) [MSC v.1914 32 b
it (Intel)] on win32
Type "copyright", "credits" or "license()" for more information.
>>>
= RESTART: C:/Users/machost/Desktop/Python_examples/python_program_12_16
.py =
x= [1 3 5 6 7]
y= [2 4 5 5 0]
x-y= [-1 -1  0  1  7]
x*y= [ 2 12 25 30  0]

Warning (from warnings module):
  File "C:/Users/machost/Desktop/Python_examples/python_program_12_16.py
", line 9
    print("x/y=", x/y)
RuntimeWarning: divide by zero encountered in true_divide
x/y= [0.5  0.75 1.   1.2   inf]
>>>
                                                        Ln: 15 Col: 4
```

Figure 12.21. Performing more elementwise operations

We can also apply the same operation to the individual elements of an array like multiplying all elements by 2 or adding a constant to all elements:

```python
import numpy as np
x=np.array([1,3,5,6,7])
y=np.array([2,4,5,5,0])
print("x=", x)
print("y=", y)
print("2*x=", 2*x)
print("y+4=", y+4)
```

The results of these operations are as follows:

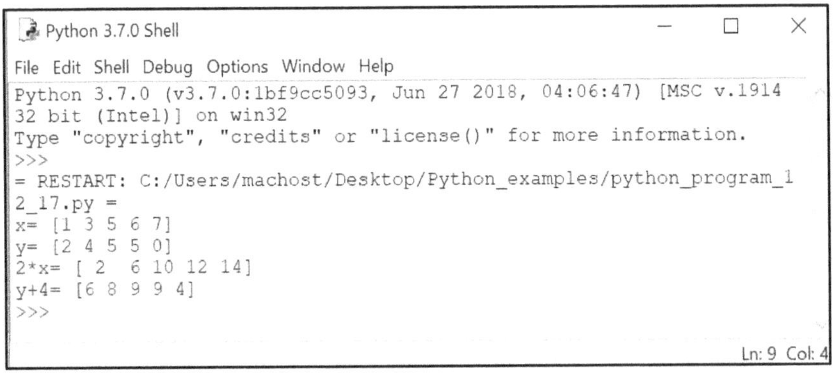

Figure 12.22. Performing multiplication and addition with constants

More advanced mathematical operations can be applied to individual elements, too. We use the methods built-in the numpy module for these type of operations like taking the exponentials of an array:

```python
import numpy as np
x=np.array([1,3,5,6,7])
print("x=", x)
print("e^x=", np.exp(x))
```

We access the exponential function by the usual dot notation as np.exp() and give the array as the parameter to this method:

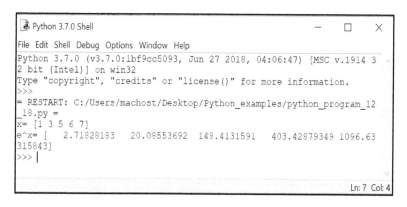

Figure 12.23. Using the built-in exponential function of the numpy library

There are numerous methods in the numpy module and we don't need to try to learn them at once, instead we can easily refer to them via the numpy page at https://docs.scipy.org/doc/numpy-1.13.0/reference/routines.math.html.

We have learned to use numpy arrays for fast mathematical processing in Python in this chapter. We will learn to visualize these data in the next chapter, after competing the exercises given below.

12.5 Exercises

1. Create the square matrix given below in Python and then calculate the inverse of this matrix using the inv() method of the numpy module.

$$A = \begin{bmatrix} 3 & 2 & 0 \\ 4 & 4 & 2 \\ 0 & 1 & 20 \end{bmatrix}$$

2. Create a vector whose elements are the angles between 0 and 360 degrees (use the arange or linspace methods) and then calculate the expression

$$\sin^2(x) + \cos^2(x)$$

where x is the individual elements of the angle vector. You can use the sin() and cos() methods of the numpy library.

3. Take a number from the user and calculate its tangent function by the tan() method of the numpy module. Then, calculate the tangent as sin/cos using the sin() and cos() methods of the numpy module. Compare the obtained values.

4. Take 16 numbers from the user and construct a 4x4 matrix from these numbers.

5. Calculate the determinant of the 5x5 eye matrix in numpy.

Chapter 13. 2D and 3D Plotting in Python – the *matplotlib* library

13.1. Introduction

Plotting data is an indispensible tool for telling the variation of the data to the user. Fortunately, Python has several plotting libraries which have their own strengths. In this book, we will learn the widely used *matplotlib* library. The command structure of the matplotlib library is similar to those of the widely used commercial mathematical programs and this provides an advantage.

13.2. Installing *matplotlib*

We will use the pip package manager of Python for installing matplotlib. Please refer to chapter 12.2 for opening the PowerShell and navigating to the Scripts folder in the shell. And then we will use the following command for initiating the installation of matplotlib:

.\pip install matplotlib

After pressing Enter on th keyboard, the installation of matplotlib will start as follows:

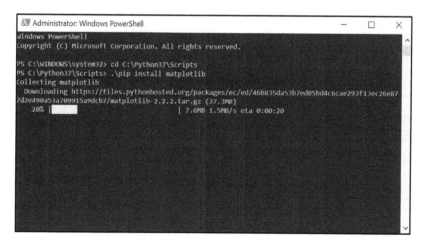

Figure 13.1. Installing matplotlib

We can test our installation by importing the matplotlib in the IDLE prompt:

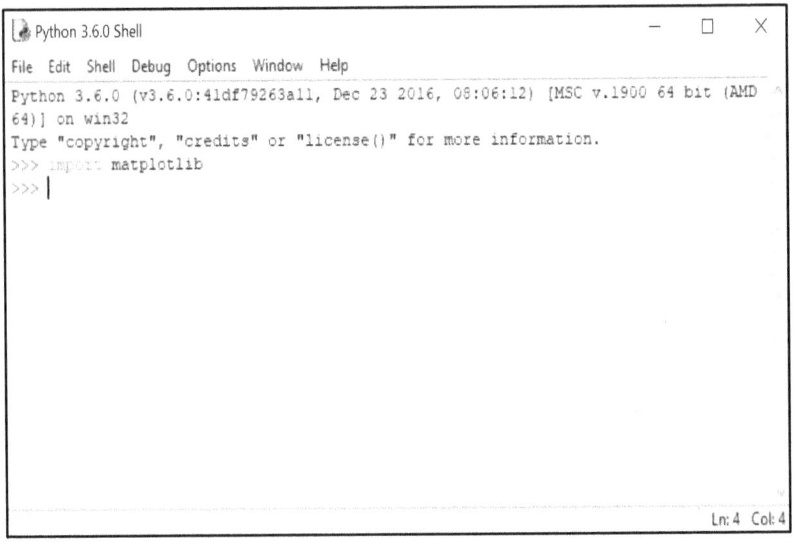

Figure 13.2. Testing our matplotlib installation

If the IDLE imports without any problems, we are ready to use matplotlib. If IDLE gives an error, please try to update your pip packaga manager by .\pip instal --upgrade pip command and then try to re-install the matplotlib package by the command given at the beginning of this chapter.

13.3. Basic 2D plotting using *matplotlib*

First of all, we will plot the variation of the elements of a list. The list contains the velocity of a car in km/h as follows:

```
velocity=[56, 60, 62, 65, 58]
```

In order to plot these values in a 2D matplotlib plot, we first need to import the *pyplot* module of the matplotlib package:

```
import matplotlib.pyplot as plt
```

Then, we will use the `plot()` method of the pyplot module:

```
plt.plot(velocity)
```

We finally need to actually show the plot on the screen:

```
plt.show()
```

Collecting these code lines, we have our first plotting program:

```
import matplotlib.pyplot as plt

velocity=[56, 60, 62, 65, 58]
plt.plot(velocity)
plt.show()
```

We get our plot on the screen when we run this program:

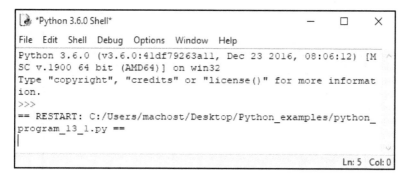

Figure 13.3. Running our first plotting program

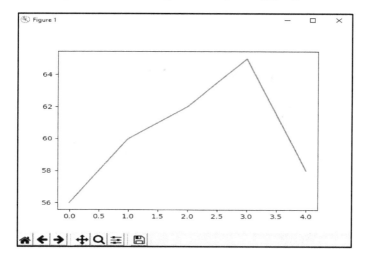

Figure 13.4. Our first plot

Note that our program will be still running when the plot is open (as seen on Figure 13.3). The program will end when we close the plot.

We can also place labels on the plot to tell more to the user as follows:

```python
import matplotlib.pyplot as plt

velocity=[56, 60, 62, 65, 58]
plt.plot(velocity)
plt.xlabel("Data number")
plt.ylabel("Velocity (km/h)")
plt.show()
```

Let's run the program again to see the new plot:

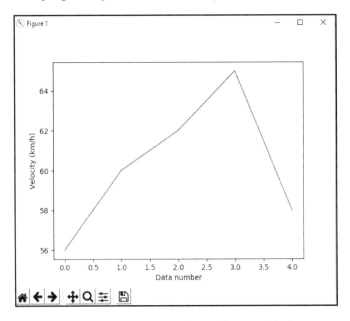

Figure 13.5. Updated plot with axes labels

13.4. Figure controls

Matplotlib plot has some controls at the bottm left corner of the figure window:

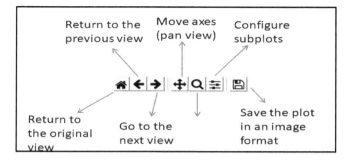

Figure 13.6. The default plot controls

The button names given in Figure 13.6. Is pretty self-explanatory. For example, we can zoom the figure using the pan view button. Click on that button and use the right mosue key to drag the plot and see if you can zoom in x and/or y axes as follows:

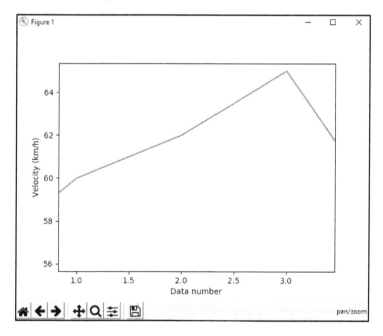

Figure 13.7. Zoomed plot

We can always click on the Home button to return to the original view:

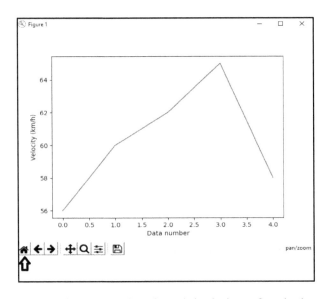

Figure 13.8. The plot returned to the original view after the home button is clicked

13.5. Plotting related vectors in *matplotlib*

We can also plot the graph of two related quantities such as time and a sine wave whose amplitude changes with time. Let's use the numpy arrays to define a time (t) vector and generate a sine wave vector (sin_t) from this vector:

```python
import numpy as np

pi=np.pi # The pi number
f=10 # Frequency of the sine wave
t=np.arange(0, 1, 1e-3) # Time vector
sin_t=np.sin(2*pi*f*t) # Sine vector
```

Noe that the time-dependent mathematical expression of the sine wave is given as:

$$x(t) = \sin(2\pi ft)$$

therefore we defined and used the pi number and a dummy frequency of f=10Hz. Let's plot this wave using matplotlib:

```
import matplotlib.pyplot as plt
import numpy as np

pi=np.pi # The pi number
f=10 # Frequency of the sine wave
t=np.arange(0, 1, 1e-3) # Time vector
sin_t=np.sin(2*pi*f*t) # Sine vector

plt.plot(t, sin_t)
plt.xlabel("Time (seconds)")
plt.ylabel("Sine value")
plt.show()
```

We have given the independent variable t and the dependent variable sin_t in order as the parameters of the plot() method: `plt.plot(t, sin_t)`. Let's see the output of this program:

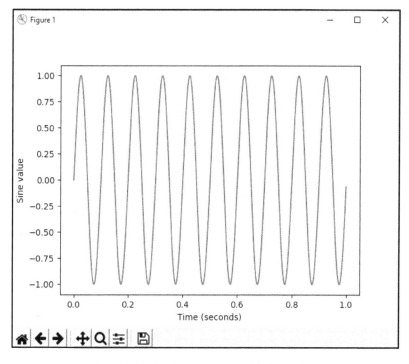

Figıre 13.9 Plotting a sinusoidal function

13.6. Changing plot properties

We can change the colour and the style of matplotlib plots by specifying the corresponding parameters in the plot() method. For changing the colour, we give the `color` parameter as follows:

```python
import matplotlib.pyplot as plt
import numpy as np

pi=np.pi # The pi number
f=10 # Frequency of the sine wave
t=np.arange(0, 1, 1e-3) # Time vector
sin_t=np.sin(2*pi*f*t) # Sine vector

plt.plot(t, sin_t, color='green')
plt.xlabel("Time (seconds)")
plt.ylabel("Sine value")
plt.show()
```

The colour of the sine plot has changed to green (you can see the colour images online at the book's website: www.yamaclis.com/python):

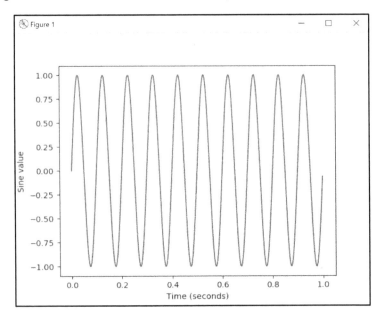

Figure 13.10. Changing the plot colour

Accepted colour parameters are: 'blue', 'orange', 'green', 'red', 'purple', 'brown', 'pink', 'grey', 'olive', 'cyan'. If you need to specify a different colour, you can also use the RGB string of your preferred colour. You can look for the RGB code of infinite colours online at, for example, https://www.rapidtables.com/web/color/RGB_Color.html.

Another property you might want to change is the line sytle, especially if you have more than one plot on the same figure. We use the `ls` parameter to change the linestyle as follows:

```
import matplotlib.pyplot as plt
import numpy as np

pi=np.pi # The pi number
f=10 # Frequency of the sine wave
t=np.arange(0, 1, 1e-3) # Time vector
sin_t=np.sin(2*pi*f*t) # Sine vector

plt.plot(t, sin_t, color='green', ls='--')
plt.xlabel("Time (seconds)")
plt.ylabel("Sine value")
plt.show()
```

We have given the `ls='--'` parameter and our linestyle will be as follows:

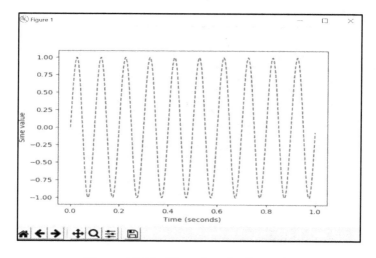

Figure 13.11. Changing the linestyle

217

The accepted linestyles in matplotlib are: ':', '-.', '--' and '-'.

Another property we can change is the line width, given as lw. The default value is 1 and we can change it by using as a parameter in the plot() method as follows:

```python
import matplotlib.pyplot as plt
import numpy as np

pi=np.pi # The pi number
f=10 # Frequency of the sine wave
t=np.arange(0, 1, 1e-3) # Time vector
sin_t=np.sin(2*pi*f*t) # Sine vector

plt.plot(t, sin_t, color='green', lw='4')
plt.xlabel("Time (seconds)")
plt.ylabel("Sine value")
plt.show()
```

And we have a thick curve:

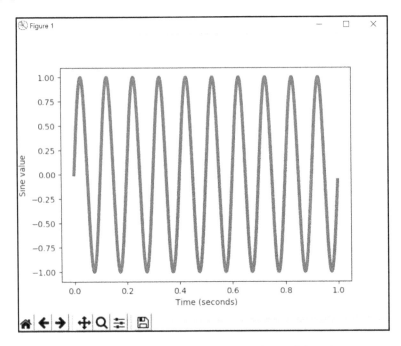

Figure 13.12. Changing the line width of the plot

The data points are not shown on the plot by default. We can display them if we specify markers for these data using the `marker` parameter:

```python
import matplotlib.pyplot as plt
import numpy as np

pi=np.pi # The pi number
f=10 # Frequency of the sine wave
t=np.arange(0, 1, 1e-3) # Time vector
sin_t=np.sin(2*pi*f*t) # Sine vector

plt.plot(t, sin_t, marker='*')
plt.xlabel("Time (seconds)")
plt.ylabel("Sine value")
plt.show()
```

The data points will be marked by *:

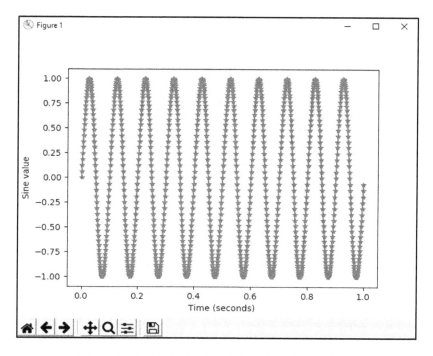

Figure 13.13. Displaying data points by markers

We can also change the default marker size using the `markersize` parameter. The default value of markersize is 5 and if we change it to **8**, the data markers will be bigger:

```python
import matplotlib.pyplot as plt
import numpy as np

pi=np.pi # The pi number
f=10 # Frequency of the sine wave
t=np.arange(0, 1, 1e-3) # Time vector
sin_t=np.sin(2*pi*f*t) # Sine vector

plt.plot(t, sin_t, marker='*', markersize=8)
plt.xlabel("Time (seconds)")
plt.ylabel("Sine value")
plt.show()
```

This is the updated plot:

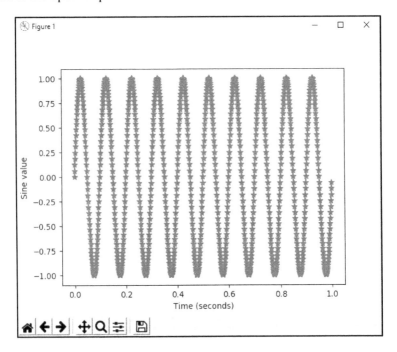

Figure 13.14. Increasing the marker size

13.7. Multiple plots on the same axes

Until now, we have plotted a single function but matplotlib lets us to plot infinte number of plots on the same axes. We just specify each x, y consequtively in the plot() method. For example, let's define two sine waves with different frequencies and then plot them on the same axes:

```python
import matplotlib.pyplot as plt
import numpy as np

pi=np.pi # The pi number
t=np.arange(0, 1, 1e-3) # Time vector

f1=2 # Frequency of the first sine wave
f2=5 # Frequency of the second sine wave

sin1_t=np.sin(2*pi*f1*t) # The first sine vector
sin2_t=np.sin(2*pi*f2*t) # The second sine vector

plt.plot(t, sin1_t, t, sin2_t)
plt.xlabel("Time (seconds)")
plt.ylabel("Sine values")
plt.show()
```

We have defined two sine vectors: sin1_t and sin2_t. Then we plotted them using the plot() method:

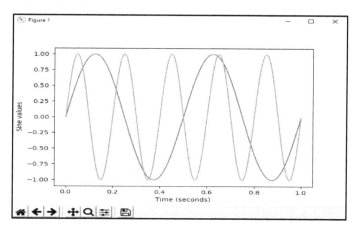

Figure 13.15. Plotting two vectors on the same axes

It is better to use legends if we have multiple plots on the same axes. We use the `legend()` method applied to our plot handle as follows:

```python
import matplotlib.pyplot as plt
import numpy as np

pi=np.pi # The pi number
t=np.arange(0, 1, 1e-3) # Time vector

f1=2 # Frequency of the first sine wave
f2=5 # Frequency of the second sine wave

sin1_t=np.sin(2*pi*f1*t) # The first sine vector
sin2_t=np.sin(2*pi*f2*t) # The second sine vector

plt.plot(t, sin1_t, t, sin2_t)
plt.legend(("f=2Hz", "f=5Hz"))
plt.xlabel("Time (seconds)")
plt.ylabel("Sine values")
plt.show()
```

Note that we provide the legend parameter as a tuple as `("f=2Hz", "f=5Hz")` in the `legend()` method. Our plot with legends will appear as follows:

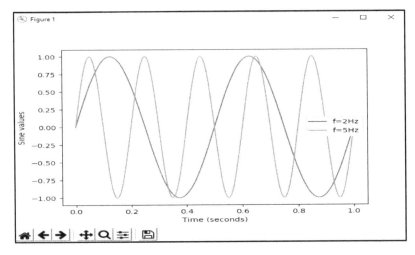

Figure 13.16. Displaying legends in a plot

13.8. Dividing the plot window - subplots

We can also divide a plot window as a table. We use the subplot() method to specify the number of rows and coloumns and to command which section to use for the current plot. Let's display our two sine waves in two different sections in the plot window:

```python
import matplotlib.pyplot as plt
import numpy as np

pi=np.pi # The pi number
t=np.arange(0, 1, 1e-3) # Time vector

f1=2 # Frequency of the first sine wave
f2=5 # Frequency of the second sine wave

sin1_t=np.sin(2*pi*f1*t) # The first sine vector
sin2_t=np.sin(2*pi*f2*t) # The second sine vector

plt.subplot(211)
plt.plot(t, sin1_t)
plt.xlabel("Time (seconds)")
plt.ylabel("Value")
plt.title("Sine wave with f=2Hz")

plt.subplot(212)
plt.plot(t, sin2_t)
plt.xlabel("Time (seconds)")
plt.ylabel("Value")
plt.title("Sine wave with f=5Hz")

plt.show()
```

The command **plt.subplot(211)** means "divide the plot window to 2 rows and 1 coloumn. And use the first section (row=1, coloumn=1) for the upcoming plot". Similarly, the command **plt.subplot(212)** means "divide the plot window to 2 rows and 1 coloumn. And use the second section (row=2, coloumn=1) for the upcoming plot". Also note that we used the title() method for setting the titles of each plot. (We can use the title() method in single plots too). Let's see what Python shows us when we run this program:

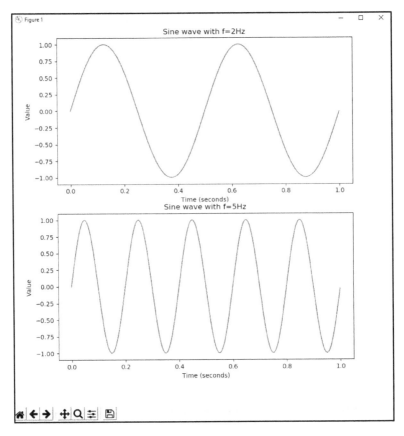

Figure 13.17. Displaying plots as a table in a single window

We have seen different variations to visualise data in 2D. We are now ready to upgrade to 3D graphs in the next section.

13.9. Plotting 3D surface graphs in *matplotlib*

3D plots are especially useful for plotting phenomena with time-varying properties. First of all, we need to import the required modules:

```
from mpl_toolkits.mplot3d import Axes3D
import matplotlib.pyplot as plt
import numpy as np
```

The first command imports the Axes3D module, which will aloow us to plot 3D graphics. The next line imports the usual pyplot module of the matplotlib package and the last line imports the numpy module for generating the x, y and z data. Let's generate x, y and z data as follows:

```
x=np.arange(-2, 2, 0.02)
y=np.arange(-2, 2, 0.02)
x, y=np.meshgrid(x, y)
z=x**2 + y**2
```

In the first line we generate linearly spaced x points from -2 to 2 with 0.02 spacing. The next line generates the y vector in the same manner. (They don't need to be the same in general). The third command creates x, y pairs for spotting points on the x-y axis using the mechgrid() method of numpy. And finally, we generate the z points according to the following function:

$$z = x^2 + y^2$$

Note that this function is just an example. We have impırted the required libraries and generated the data. We are now ready to plot the z points as a function of x and y:

```
fig=plt.figure()
ax=fig.gca(projection='3d')
surf=ax.plot_surface(x, y, z)
plt.show()
```

The first line creates a figure object using the figure() method. The next line converts the current figure to a 3D capable object and the third line actually plots z as the function of x and y using the plot_surface() method. The last line displays the graphics on the screen. The whole program and its output is shown below:

```
from mpl_toolkits.mplot3d import Axes3D
import matplotlib.pyplot as plt
import numpy as np

x=np.arange(-2, 2, 0.02)
y=np.arange(-2, 2, 0.02)
x, y=np.meshgrid(x, y)
z=x**2 + y**2
```

```
fig=plt.figure()
ax=fig.gca(projection='3d')
surf=ax.plot_surface(x, y, z)
plt.show()
```

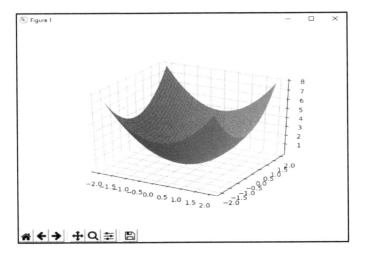

Figure 13.18. Our first 3D plot

We can drag and rotate the surface plot using the left mouse button:

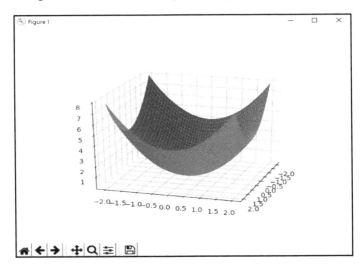

Figure 13.19. Rotated plot

13.10. Adding labels and titles to the 3D plot

We can also add labels to the x, y and z axes and also a title as in the 2D case:

```python
from mpl_toolkits.mplot3d import Axes3D
import matplotlib.pyplot as plt
import numpy as np

x=np.arange(-2, 2, 0.02)
y=np.arange(-2, 2, 0.02)
x, y=np.meshgrid(x, y)
z=x**2 + y**2

fig=plt.figure()
ax=fig.gca(projection='3d')
surf=ax.plot_surface(x, y, z)

ax.set_xlabel("x")
ax.set_ylabel("y")
ax.set_zlabel("z")
ax.set_title("3D plot")

plt.show()
```

The updated graph will be as follows:

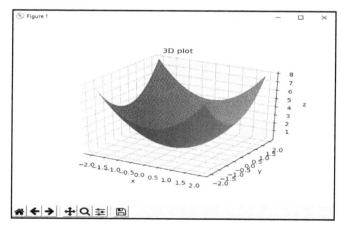

Figure 13.20. Adding labels and title to the 3D plot

13.11. Adding a colourmap and colourbar to the 3D plot

It is also possible to plot the 3D graphs with a colormap, which means colouring the data according to its current value. We use the cm module of the matplotlib library for this and provide a colourmap parameter in the surface_plot() method as follows:

```
from mpl_toolkits.mplot3d import Axes3D
import matplotlib.pyplot as plt
import numpy as np
from matplotlib import cm

x=np.arange(-2, 2, 0.02)
y=np.arange(-2, 2, 0.02)
x, y=np.meshgrid(x, y)
z=x**2 + y**2

fig=plt.figure()
ax=fig.gca(projection='3d')
surf=ax.plot_surface(x, y, z, cmap=cm.coolwarm)

ax.set_xlabel("x")
ax.set_ylabel("y")
ax.set_zlabel("z")
ax.set_title("3D plot")

plt.show()
```

The plot will be a coloured one in this case as shown in Figure 13.21.

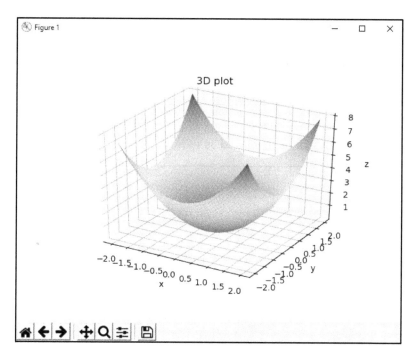

Figure 13.21. Adding a colourmap (coloured figure online at www.yamaclis.com/python)

Finally, we can add a colourbar which shows the clours and coorresponding values using the colorbar() method as follows:

```python
from mpl_toolkits.mplot3d import Axes3D
import matplotlib.pyplot as plt
import numpy as np
from matplotlib import cm

x=np.arange(-2, 2, 0.02)
y=np.arange(-2, 2, 0.02)
x, y=np.meshgrid(x, y)
z=x**2 + y**2

fig=plt.figure()
ax=fig.gca(projection='3d')
surf=ax.plot_surface(x, y, z, cmap=cm.coolwarm)
fig.colorbar(surf)

ax.set_xlabel("x")
```

```
ax.set_ylabel("y")
ax.set_zlabel("z")
ax.set_title("3D plot")

plt.show()
```

The new 3D plot will be displayed as follows:

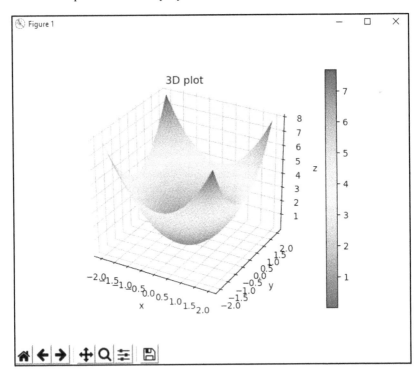

Figure 13.22. Plotting with a colourbar

We have completed our plotting chapter and now you have learned plotting 2D and 3D graphics with nice decorations like labels, titles and colourbars. Next chapter will also be an exciting chapter because we will learn developing graphical user interfaces (GUIs) for our Python programs which will enable us to distribute our software to wider audiences. But please try to complete the exercises section below before advancing to the next chapter.

13.12. Exercises

1. Write a program to plot the function $f(x) = x^3 + x$ for x in the range of -1 to 1 with 0.001 spacing. Don't forget to place appropriate labels and a title.

2. Write a program to plot two 2D plots in the same window using subplot(121) and subplot(122) and observe what these commands will produce.

3. Write a program to plot the surface plot of $f(x, y) = x \cdot y + x + y$ with x and y in the range of 0 to 5 with 0.002 spacings.

4. Write a program to plot the temperature vs day of the current month of the place you live (you can use www.accuweather.com for the data).

5. Write a program to draw a cardioid (heart) in Python (you'll need to explore the Internet for finding its function).

Part IV. Developing Desktop Apps in Python

Chapter 14. Graphical User Interfaces in Python – the *tkinter* library

14.1. Introduction

Presenting your software with a graphical user interface (GUI) is generally a must because 1) the general user is accustomed to GUIs and 2) you can show your program's options in the best way possible with GUIs. There are several GUI libraries, free and paid, available in Python. We will learn the tkinter GUI library in this book because it is mature, free, ships with Python and available for all major operating systems. Therefore, if you develop your GUI with tkinter, you can ship your software to anyone without dealing with license issues or operating system compatibility.

14.2. Short history of *tkinter*

Tkinter is a binding to the Tk toolkit. Tk is a free tookit that provides GUI elements. Tk itself is developed in C programming language by the Tcl/Tk team but the tkinter library allows us to use Tk GUI system with simple Python commands. (Tk is orignally combined with the Tcl programming language named as Tcl/Tk, which is still widely used today for its simple syntax). The good news is that the standard Python installer comes with the tkinter library therefore if you have installed Python as shown in Chapter 2, you don't need to install anything else. We can simply start developing our GUIs in Python.

14.3. Creating the main window

The simplest GUI program consists of the following program in Python:

```
import tkinter as tk

window=tk.Tk()
window.mainloop()
```

In the first line, we import the tkinter module as tk. In the next command, we call the constructor method of tkinter Tk(), which creates an empty window with the default size of 200x200 pixels. And the last line contains a very important command, it makes the window actually appear on the screen waiting with the main event loop. The main event loop listens to mouse and keyboard movements like clicking a button or entering a text. Let's run this program and see its output as in Figure 14.1.

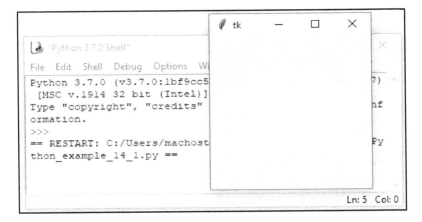

Figure 14.1. Our first GUI window in Python

14.4. Adding an app icon and an app title

Our first GUI window has the default title "tk" and the defayult icon as a feather as you can see from Figure 14.1. We can easily change these properties. We can use a Python icon file as supplied in the book's website (www.yamaclis.com/python) named python.ico and a title of "My GUI window" with the code below:

```
import tkinter as tk

window=tk.Tk()
window.iconbitmap('python.ico')
window.title("My GUI Window")
window.mainloop()
```

We have used the iconbitmap() and title() methods applied to our window handler. Let's see our updated GUI window by executing this program:

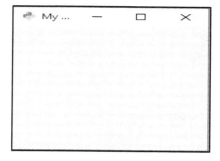

Figure 14.2. Changing the icon and title defaults

14.5. Changing the initial window size

The window's title is not displayed properly in Figure 14.2. as the width of the window is not enough. We can set the default window size of the tkinter with the geometry() method. We give the initial size as as string inside this method as follows:

```
import tkinter as tk

window=tk.Tk()
window.iconbitmap('python.ico')
window.title("My GUI Window")
window.geometry("400x400")
window.mainloop()
```

The window will be opened 400x400 pixels as shown in Figure 14.13.

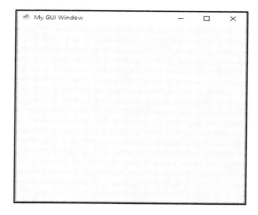

Figure 14.3. Setting the initial size of the window

14.6. Resizing permissions

We can also set the resizing permissions of the window. We use the resizable() method for this. The parameters of this method are two booleans which specify if the window is permitted to be resized in x and y directions. For example, if we set bthe parameters as 0, 0 the window will not be resizable in either x or y direction. The maximize button of the window will also be inactivated in this case:

```
import tkinter as tk

window=tk.Tk()
window.iconbitmap('python.ico')
window.title("My GUI Window")
window.geometry("400x400")
window.resizable(0, 0)
window.mainloop()
```

We will not be able to change the size of the window in this case:

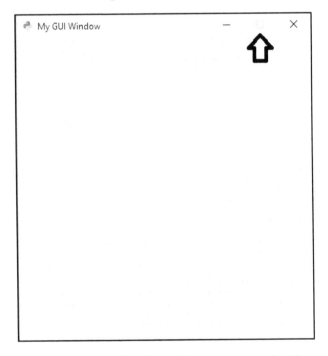

Figure 14.4. Setting the window as non-resizable

14.7. The *Label* widget

Tkinter offers a complete set of GUI objects and these are called as tkinter widgets, or just widgets (without just!). The first and basic widget we will use is the Label widget of the themed tkinter library. The widgets of tkinter are nice but the themed tkinter "ttk" library provides a widget set that is more similar to the operating system's own componnets. Therefore we will use the themed widgets of ttk in this book. We just add a Label using the Label() method of the ttk library as follows:

```
import tkinter as tk
from tkinter import ttk

window=tk.Tk()

my_label=ttk.Label(window, text="My first
                    Label...")

window.mainloop()
```

We firstly imported the ttk module from the tkinter package in the second line. And after creating the main window, we created a Label widget called my_label by its constructor method Label() of the ttk class. Note that the Label() method accepts the parent container (window object in this example) and its text as its parameters. When we run this program, we will see a window like below:

Figure 14.5. The output of our program

Where is the label? The window does not has the Label widget because we didn't specify where to place the Label in our program. Because of this Python didn't draw the Label in the window. We have three options to specify the positions of widgets in a window and the simplest of these methods is the pack() method. It just packs the widgets, i.e. it places the widgets from top to down in a window in the order they are defined.

```python
import tkinter as tk
from tkinter import ttk

window=tk.Tk()

my_label=ttk.Label(window, text="My first
label...")
my_label.pack()

window.mainloop()
```

The Label widget will be packed in the window and will apppear a follows in this program:

Figure 14.6. Our first widget in the window

Note that the window is automatically resized according to the size of the Label widget. Let's add another label to our program and pack it also:

```python
import tkinter as tk
from tkinter import ttk
window=tk.Tk()

my_label=ttk.Label(window, text="My first
label...")
my_label.pack()

new_label=ttk.Label(window, text="Another label.")
new_label.pack()
window.mainloop()
```

Our program with these two Label widgets will be as follows:

Figure 14.7. The two Label widgets packed in the window

The pack() method doesn't provide much control over the layout of the widgets in the window therefore we will use other methods that will be explained in a short while. But for now, let's see more properties of Labels before passing to the layout managers.

We can use the config() method to configure the properties of Labels after their definition. Let's study the following example code:

```python
import tkinter as tk
from tkinter import ttk

window=tk.Tk()

my_label=ttk.Label(window, text="My first label...")
my_label.pack()

my_label.config(text="New text.")
my_label.config(foreground="white",
background="blue")
my_label.config(font=('Arial', 44, "bold"))

window.mainloop()
```

We have changed the text of the Label and then set its foreground (text) and the background colours. Finally, we changed the font style and size. We get the following window with this program:

Figure 14.8. Label with updated properties

Finally, let's put an image to our label (we'll use the label.png image supplied on the book's website):

```
import tkinter as tk
from tkinter import ttk

window=tk.Tk()

my_label=ttk.Label(window, text="My first
label...")
my_label.pack()

my_label.config(text="New text.")
my_label.config(foreground="black",
background="white")
my_label.config(font=('Arial', 14, "bold"))

image_icon=tk.PhotoImage(file="label.png")
my_label.config(image=image_icon)
my_label.config(compound="text")
my_label.config(compound="center")

window.mainloop()
```

Note that the image file should be in the same directory as our Python file otherwise we should need to specify the relative path to the file. The PhotoImage() method creates an image handle of the "label.png" image file. The following three command lines set the image of the label to be this image, and then draws the text and the image both centered on the Label widget. The output is as follows:

Figure 14.9. Adding an image to the Label and displaying the image and the text together

We frequently use the images alone in the Label widget in applications rather than using image and text together.

That's all for Labels for now. Let's study the layout managers grid() and place() in the next chapter.

14.8. Layout managers: *pack()*, *grid()* and *place()*

The tkinter library has three types of layout managers: pack(), grid() and place(). We have already used the pack manager, it just stacks all the widgets on top of each other therefore not very suitable for professional applications. Therefore we will start with the grid() manager here. The grid() manager divides the window to virtual grids and places the given widget to the cell specified by the row and column parameters. For example, we can imagine our window to be divided into four grids as follows:

row=0, column=0	row=0, column=1
row=1, column=0	row=1, column=1

The functionality of grid() is not limited to 2x2 grids only, it can divide the window to any number of grids as we need. Let's create a window and place 4 Labels using a 2x2 grid:

```
import tkinter as tk
from tkinter import ttk

window=tk.Tk()

label_1=ttk.Label(window, text="This is label 1")
label_2=ttk.Label(window, text="This is label 2")
```

243

```
label_3=ttk.Label(window, text="This is label 3")
label_4=ttk.Label(window, text="This is label 4")

label_1.grid(row=0, column=0)
label_2.grid(row=0, column=1)
label_3.grid(row=1, column=0)
label_4.grid(row=1, column=1)

window.mainloop()
```

The labels will be placed in a virtual grid:

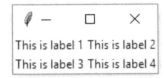

Figure 14.10. Using the grid() manager

Let's colour the backgrounds of the labels to see the grids easily:

```
import tkinter as tk
from tkinter import ttk

window=tk.Tk()

label_1=ttk.Label(window, text="This is label 1",
background="yellow")
label_2=ttk.Label(window, text="This is label 2",
background="blue")
label_3=ttk.Label(window, text="This is label 3",
background="green")
label_4=ttk.Label(window, text="This is label 4",
background="white")

label_1.grid(row=0, column=0)
label_2.grid(row=0, column=1)
label_3.grid(row=1, column=0)
label_4.grid(row=1, column=1)

window.mainloop()
```

Now, the grids can be seen as follows:

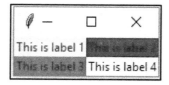

Figure 14.11. The grids in colour (colour figure online at
www.yamaclis.com/python)

Please note that we can use the grid() layout manager for any widget, not just for labels.

The last layout alternative is the place() manager. In place() manager, we specify the exact locations of the widgets in pixels considering the window as a canvas. Let's specify the location of a label using the place() method:

```python
import tkinter as tk
from tkinter import ttk

window=tk.Tk()
window.geometry("600x400")

label_1=ttk.Label(window, background="red",
foreground="white", text="Label 1")
label_1.place(x=150, y=150)

window.mainloop()
```

We created a window of 600x400 pixels and then placed label_1 widget at the x=150px and y=150px. This means the top left corner of the widget will be 150px down and 150px right to the top left corner of the window:

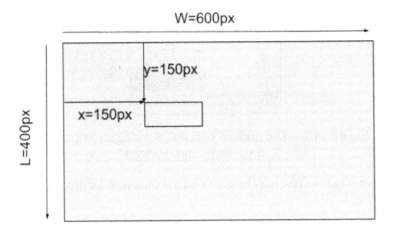

Figure 14.12. Layout of the window

Let's run our program to see the output:

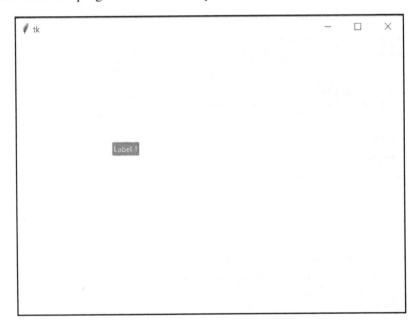

Figure 14.13. Using the place() layout manager to place a label

Please note that the location of the label will not change as we resize the window as we used *absoulte pixel locations* x=150px and y=150px for the label:

Figure 14.14. Resizing the window does not change the position of the label

It is also possible to use the place() manager with *relative locations* with relx and relx keywords. In this context, relx=0.5 means place the top left corner of the widget starting at the 50% th pixel of the width of the current window size. Similarly, rely=0.3 means to place the top left corner at the 30% th pixel of the height of the window. Let's modify our example to use relative positions:

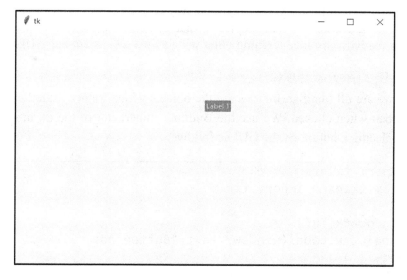

Figure 14.15. Using the relative positions

When we use the relative positions, the position of the label is automatically scaled when we change the window size:

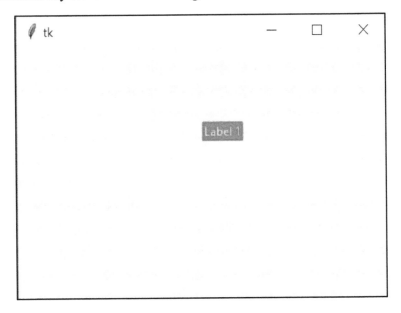

Figure 14.16. Scaling the window also scales the position of the label

We now know all three layout managers: pack(), grid() and place(). The grid() manager is the popular one because it provides more professional looking and robust layouts therefore, we will use this manager in the following sections of this chapter so that you can get used to it. We are now ready to continue learning other widgets we will use in our GUIs.

14.9. The *Button* widget

As we are all familiar, buttons are the objects which trigger something to happen when clicked. We use the Button() constructor of the ttk module for placing a button on the GUI as follows:

```
import tkinter as tk
from tkinter import ttk

window=tk.Tk()
label=ttk.Label(window, text="Button not clicked
yet...")
label.grid(row=0, column=0)
```

```
def change_button():
    label.config(text="Button is clicked.")

button=ttk.Button(window, text="Click me",
command=change_button)
button.grid(row=0, column=1)

window.mainloop()
```

We have defined a label before the button. And we will change the label's text when the button is clicked. For this, we define a function called change_button(). This function will be executed when the button is clicked as the command parameter of the Button() constructor is set as this function with **command=change_button**. We have used the grid() layout manager to display the button and the label next to each other in the GUI window. Let's execute this program to see its output:

Figure 14.17. GUI with a button

When we click the button, the label's text will be changed with the change_button() function

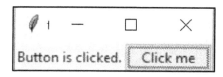

Figure 14.18. The GUI after the button is clicked

14.10. The *Checkbutton* widget

Checkbuttons operate similar to checkboxes we use in webforms that we check to agree terms and conditions, for example when we are registering for a subscriptions online. The usage of checkbuttons are similar to those of buttons with some extended functionality. We can check the state of the Checkbuttons using auxiliary (aux) variables of the tkinter package as follows:

```
import tkinter as tk
from tkinter import ttk

window=tk.Tk()

label=ttk.Label(window, text="Checkbutton
unchecked.")
label.grid(row=0, column=1)

Checkbutton_state=tk.BooleanVar()

def check():
    if(Checkbutton_state.get() == True):
        label.config(text="Agreed")
    else:
        label.config(text="Not agreed")

checkbutton=ttk.Checkbutton(window, text="Agree?",
variable=Checkbutton_state, command=check)

checkbutton.grid(row=0, column=0)

window.mainloop()
```

Here we firstly define an aux variable Checkbutton_state having the tkinter type BooleanVar(). The state of the Checkbutton will be stored in this variable. Then, we define a function called check() which will modify the Label's text according to the value of the Checkbutton_state variable. If the Checkbutton is checked, this will set the value of the Checkbutton_state as True. Similarly, is the Checkbutton is unchecked, the value of this BooleanVar will be False. This is checked using the get() method applied on the Checkbutton_state variable and the text of the Label is set accordingly in the check() function. Finally, we create and declare the Checkbutton widget with the corresponding variable and the command. Let's execute this program to see its first state:

Figure 14.19. The initial state of the program

Let's check the Checkbutton:

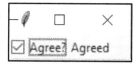

Figure 14.20.Our GUI when the Checkbutton is checked

Let's now uncheck the Checkbutton:

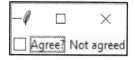

Figure 14.21. The GUI when the Checkbutton is unchecked

The Checkbuttons provide both a *command* parameter which executes when the Checkbutton is clicked (checked or unchecked) and a *variable* parameter which enables us to get the current state of the Checkbutton.

14.11. The *Radiobutton* widget

Radiobuttons work similar to Checkbuttons. The difference is that we can only check a single Radiobutton in a window while we can check multiple Checkbuttons at the same time. Let's place three Radiobuttons on a window and use a StringVar() variable to get the selected Radiobutton in our example:

```python
import tkinter as tk
from tkinter import ttk

window=tk.Tk()

label=ttk.Label(window, text="No drink selected
yet.")
label.grid(row=1, column=1)

Radiobutton_state=tk.StringVar()

def setLabel():
    if(Radiobutton_state.get() == "Tea"):
        label.config(text="Tea")
    elif(Radiobutton_state.get() == "Coffee"):
```

```
            label.config(text="Coffee")
    elif(Radiobutton_state.get() == "Lemonade"):
        label.config(text="Lemonade")

Radiobutton1=ttk.Radiobutton(window, text="Tea",
variable=Radiobutton_state, value="Tea",
command=setLabel)
Radiobutton1.grid(row=0, column=0)

Radiobutton2=ttk.Radiobutton(window, text="Coffee",
variable=Radiobutton_state, value="Coffee",
command=setLabel)
Radiobutton2.grid(row=1, column=0)

Radiobutton3=ttk.Radiobutton(window,
text="Lemonade", variable=Radiobutton_state,
value="Lemonade", command=setLabel)
Radiobutton3.grid(row=2, column=0)

window.mainloop()
```

We have declared the Radiobutton_state variable from the tkinter module. Then we placed three Radiobuttons for selecting a drink as Tea, Coffee or Lemonade. The Radiobuttons set the Radiobutton_state variable to the corresponding drink. Finally, we set the Label's text according to the value of the Radiobutton_state variable's value in the setLabel() function which is called whenever a Radiobutton is checked since the command parameters of these Radiobuttons are set as setLabel. Let's run our example:

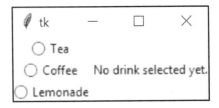

Figure 14.22. Using Radiobuttons on a GUI

When we select a drink, the Label will display the selected drink as follows:

Figure 14.23. Using Radiobuttons

Note that we can only select a single drink since we used Radiobuttons.

14.12. The *Combobox* widget

Combobox provides a list of options for the user to select. It is used when the number of possibilities are not practical to show in the window. We will now use a Combobox for providing a list of options for selecting a drink (we're modifying the Radiobutton example):

```python
import tkinter as tk
from tkinter import ttk

window=tk.Tk()

label=ttk.Label(window, text="No drink selected
yet.")
label.grid(row=0, column=1)

Combobox_value=tk.StringVar()

def setLabel(event):
    if(Combobox_value.get() == "Tea"):
        label.config(text="Tea")
    elif(Combobox_value.get() == "Coffee"):
        label.config(text="Coffee")
    elif(Combobox_value.get() == "Lemonade"):
        label.config(text="Lemonade")
    elif(Combobox_value.get()=="Water"):
        label.config(text="Water")
    elif(Combobox_value.get()=="Orange juice"):
        label.config(text="Orange juice")

combobox=ttk.Combobox(window,
textvariable=Combobox_value)
```

```
combobox.bind("<<ComboboxSelected>>", setLabel)
combobox.config(values=("Tea", "Coffee",
"Lemonade", "Water", "Orange juice"))
combobox.grid(row=0, column=0)

window.mainloop()
```

Note that we give the Combobox values as a tuple. Also note that we use the bind() method which binds a function to the ComboboxSelected event. This means that the setLabel function will be executed when this event (selecting a value from the Combobox) occurs. It is also important to give the event keyword to the binded function as a parameter (setLabel(event) in this example). Let's execute this program to observe our Combobox:

Figure 14.24. Using a Combobox

We can click on the arrow to see the options of the Combobox:

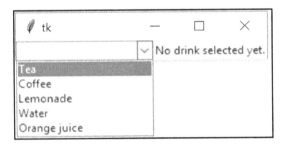

Figure 14.25. Viewing the options

When we select one of the options, the binded function will be executed changing the label accordingly:

Figure 14.26. Selecting an option from the Combobox

14.13. The *Spinbox* widget

Spinboxes are used to provide a wide range of numeric options to the user where entering them one by one to a Comboboz is not practical such as selecting the date of birth as follows:

```python
import tkinter as tk
from tkinter import ttk

window=tk.Tk()

label=ttk.Label(window, text="Date of birth not
selected yet...")
label.grid(row=0, column=1)

def setLabel():
    label.config(text= "Date of birth:" +
spinbox.get())

spinbox=tk.Spinbox(window, command=setLabel)

spinbox.config(from_ = 1930, to = 2010)
spinbox.grid(row=0, column=0)

window.mainloop()
```

First of all note that the Spinbox widget is derived from the tk package not the ttk package. Then, the limits of the spinbox values are given by the from_ and to parameters in the range of 1930 to 2010. The command parameter of the Spinbox widget sets the function to be executed when the value of theSpinbox is changed. It is the setLabel() function in this example. The value of the Spinbox is directly extracted by the get() method applied on the Spinbox widget in the setLabel() function. The program window will appear as follows:

Figure 14.27. Our program with a Spinbox widget

When we change the value of the Spinbox, the current value will be displayed on the Label:

Figure 14.28. Changing the selected value of the Spinbox

14.14. The *Entry* widget

Entry widget is used for providing the user with a text area which permits to enter a single line of text. The length of the Entry widget therefore the length of the text can be adjusted as needed. We use the get() method on the Entry widget to get the entered text as a string:

```python
import tkinter as tk
from tkinter import ttk

window=tk.Tk()

label=ttk.Label(window, text="No text entered
yet...")
label.grid(row=1, column=0)

def setLabel(event):
    label.config(text= entry.get())

entry=tk.Entry(window)
entry.grid(row=0, column=0)

entry.bind ("<Return>",setLabel)

window.mainloop()
```

We created an Entry on top of a Label widget. We binded the setLabel function to the Entry so that the setLabel() function will be run when the user hits the Return key (Enter key) on his/her keyboard after entering some text. Then, the entered text will be displayed on the Label:

Figure 14.29. Using an Entry widget

Let's enter some text in the Entry and hit Enter on the keyboard:

Figure 14.30. Displaying the text entered in the Entry widget

14.15. The *Text* widget

The Text widget operates similar to the Entry widget except the Text widget accepts text with multiple lines and we can use scrollbars in the Text widget. Here's out Text widget example, modified from the Entry widget example:

```python
import tkinter as tk
from tkinter import ttk

window=tk.Tk()

label=ttk.Label(window, text="No text entered
yet...")
label.grid(row=1, column=0)

def setLabel(event):
    label.config(text= text_entry.get("1.0",
"end"))

text_entry=tk.Text(window, width=20, height=10)
text_entry.grid(row=0, column=0)

text_entry.bind ("<Return>",setLabel)

window.mainloop()
```

Note that we defined the width and height of the Text widget in its constructor method as width=20 and height=10. Also note that we need to specify the index of the text to be taken from the Text widget in the get() method. Here, get("1.0", "end") means we want to take the whole text. Then, the text of the Text widget is written on the Label as before:

Figure 14.31. The Text widget on our GUI

Entering some text and pressing Enter makes the Label to display the whole text:

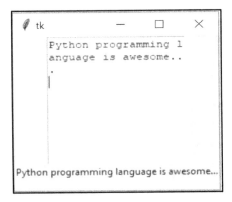

Figure 14.32. Pressing Enter to display the text on the Label

We can also use a parameter word="wrap" to wrap the words for a better experience:

```
import tkinter as tk
from tkinter import ttk
```

```
window=tk.Tk()

label=ttk.Label(window, text="No text entered
yet...")
label.grid(row=1, column=0)

def setLabel(event):
    label.config(text= text_entry.get("1.0",
"end"))

text_entry=tk.Text(window, width=20, height=10,
wrap="word")
text_entry.grid(row=0, column=0)

text_entry.bind ("<Return>",setLabel)

window.mainloop()
```

Our Text widget will now wrap the words:

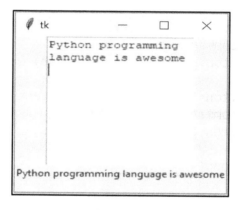

Figure 14.33. Using the word wrap property of the Text widget

14.16. The *Progressbar* widget

Progressbar widget is used for displaying the current progess of an operation. It is generally used for longer operations such as copying a large file or a heavy computation. We specify the length of the Progressbar in its constructor method as follows:

259

```
import tkinter as tk
from tkinter import ttk

window=tk.Tk()

progressbar=ttk.Progressbar(window, length=100)
progressbar.grid(row=0, column=0)

def increase_function():
    progressbar.step(10)

def start_function():
    progressbar.start()

def stop_function():
    progressbar.stop()

increase_button=ttk.Button(window, text="Increase
the progress", command=increase_function)
increase_button.grid(row=1, column=0)

increase_button=ttk.Button(window, text="Start the
progress", command=start_function)
increase_button.grid(row=2, column=0)

increase_button=ttk.Button(window, text="Stop the
progress", command=stop_function)
increase_button.grid(row=3, column=0)

window.mainloop()
```

When we click the Increase progress button, the progressbar is incremented by 10 steps. Similarly, the progressbar starts to fill automatically if we click the Start the progress buutton and stops when we click the Stop the progress button:

Figure 14.34. Increasing the Progressbar

Figure 14.35. Starting the Progressbar

Figure 14.36. Stopping the Progressbar

14.17. *Messagebox* widgets

MessageBox widgets display information to the user. We need to import the *messagebox* module from the tkinter package to use MessageBox widget as follows:

```
import tkinter as tk
from tkinter import ttk
from tkinter import messagebox

window=tk.Tk()

def show_msgbox():
    messagebox.showinfo(message="This is a simple
messagebox.", title="Msgbox")

def show_yesnocancel_msgbox():
    messagebox.askyesnocancel(message="Would you
like to have a tea?", title="Yes-No-Cancel Box")


show_msgbox_button=ttk.Button(window, text="Show a
simple messagebox", command=show_msgbox)
show_msgbox_button.grid(row=1, column=0)

show_yesnocancel_button=ttk.Button(window,
text="Show a simple yes-no-cancel messagebox",
command=show_yesnocancel_msgbox)
show_yesnocancel_button.grid(row=2, column=0)


window.mainloop()
```

We will have a simple informational messagebox and a yes, no, cancel messagebox when we click the respective buttons:

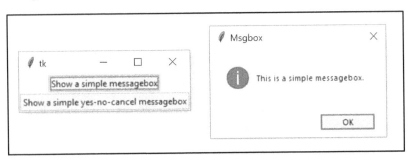

Figure 14.37. Displaying a simple MessageBox

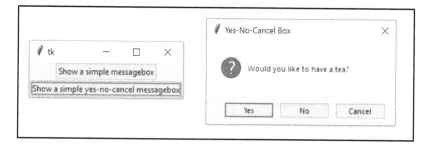

Figure 14.38. Displaying a Yes-No-Cancel MessageBox

There are six types of widely used MessageBoxes in tkinter namely OK, OKCANCEL, YESNO, YESNOCANCEL, RETRYCANCEL and ABORTRETRYIGNORE. We can use any of them as shown above.

14.18. *Filedialog* widgets

Filedialog widgets are used for providing the user with a dialog for selecting files or folders. We first need to import the filedialog module from the tkinter package and then use the appropriate method to access the file dialogs as follows:

```
import tkinter as tk
from tkinter import ttk
from tkinter import messagebox
from tkinter import filedialog

window=tk.Tk()

def open_file():
    file_name_and_path=filedialog.askopenfile()
    messagebox.showinfo(title="File info",
message=file_name_and_path.name)

file_select_button=ttk.Button(window, text="Open a
file", command=open_file)
file_select_button.grid(row=0, column=0)

window.mainloop()
```

When we click the Open a file button, the open_file() function will be run. The user will be asked to select a file with a dialog. And then, the path and the name of the selected file will be displayed in a messagebox:

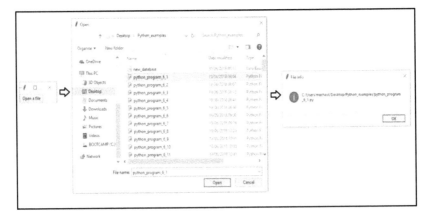

Figure 14.39. Using the openfiledialog to select a file

Once a file is selected, we can open it in Python and edit/modify as we learned in Chapter 10. Frequently used filedialog methods acan be given as askdirectory, asksaveasfile, asksaveasfilename, askopenfile and askopenfilename.

14.19. *Menu* widgets

Menu widgets lets us to add a menu and related buttons to the menu. First of all, we add a menu bar (main menu) and then add the sub sections in a hierarchical manner. The following example shows adding a main menu with File and About sections:

```python
import tkinter as tk
from tkinter import ttk
from tkinter import messagebox
from tkinter import filedialog

window=tk.Tk()

main_menu=tk.Menu(window)
window.config(menu=main_menu)

file_menu=tk.Menu(main_menu)
about_menu=tk.Menu(main_menu)

main_menu.add_cascade(menu=file_menu, label="File")
main_menu.add_cascade(menu=about_menu,
label="About")
```

```
def openfile():
    messagebox.showinfo(message="Opening a
file...")

def showabout():
    messagebox.showinfo(message="This progam is
developed by me:)")

file_menu.add_command(label="Open a File",
command=openfile)
about_menu.add_command(label="About...",
command=showabout)

window.mainloop()
```

We have added commands to the sections by the add_command()
methods similar to the method we use with buttons. Let's run our
example to see our program window:

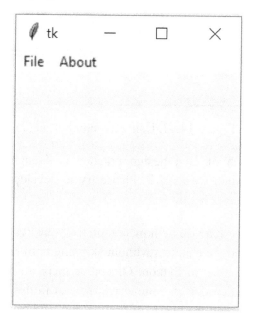

Figure 14.40. Using a menu in our program window

Let's click the File menu and then the Open a File button:

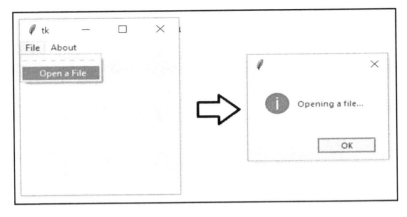

Figure 14.41. Using a menu button (1)

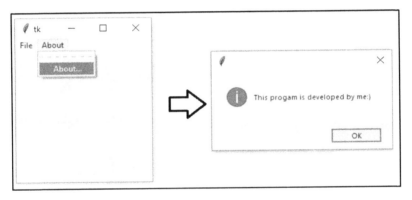

Figure 14.42. Using a menu button (2)

I think this much of GUI design practice is enough for developing standard GUIs when we need it. Please try to develop the applications given in the exercises below.

The good news is that you've now completed your Python course and if you have followed the chapters without skipping until here, you can now develop working apps in Python. Of course there are Python packages we couldn't practice due to volume restrictions in this beginner's book however you grasped the basics of Python now and can easily use other packages as you need them using various online resources. Thank you again for letting my book to help you learn the Python programming language in the Pythonic way!

14.20. Exercises

1. Write a program that has a GUI on which the user enters name, surname and age information to Entry boxes and the program saves these data on a Sqlite database.

2. Write a program that displays the data on an Sqlite database.

3. Write a number guessing program. The program will generate an integer between 1 and 20 and hide this number from the user. User will write his/her guesses in an Entry box and click a button to check if he/she guessed right. The program will display a message box tı tell the user if his/her guess was right. When the user guesses the number correctly, the program will display a congratulation message with the number of guesses he/she made until finding the number.

4. Draw a cube on a canvas in tkinter (you'll need to check the tkinter manual online).

5. Draw a sine wave on a tkinter window using the numpy and matplotlib libraries with tkinter (you'll need to check the tkinter manual online).

Epilogue

I really hope that you enjoyed this book and got some confidence for developing software in Python. If you would like to share your complaints and suggestions, please feel free to drop me an e-mail at syamacli@gmail.com or alternatively you can share it publicly on the comments section of the book's website www.yamaclis.com/python.

This book was intended to be a beginner's guide. If you have followed this book thoroughly, you should be ready to learn more on Python programming and the first source for this is, of course, the Internet. I recommend the following websites for advanced subjects on Python and tkinter:

- https://docs.python.org/3/library/tk.html
- https://matplotlib.org/api/index.html
- https://www.fullstackpython.com/databases.html

I''d like to finish this book with the following quotes which I think have deep meanings:

A wise man will make more opportunities than he finds.

Francis Bacon

Discipline strengthens the mind so that it becomes impervious to the corroding influence of fear.

Bernard Law Montgomery

Time is everything; five minutes make the difference between victory and defeat.

Horatio Nelson

References

1. https://www.python.org

2. https://sqlitestudio.pl

3. http://www.tiobe.com/tiobe-index

4. https://wiki.python.org/moin/TkInter

5. Duncan M. McGregor, Mastering matplotlib, Pack Publishing, 2015.

6. http://www.learnswift.tips/

7. Mark Roseman, Modern Tkinter for Busy Python Developers, Big Nerd Ranch Guides, 2017.

8. https://www.learnpython.org

Password for the files those can be downloaded from the book's compainon website (www.yamaclis.com/python) : **Python2019**

www.ingramcontent.com/pod-product-compliance
Lightning Source LLC
Chambersburg PA
CBHW071107050326
40690CB00008B/1142